Pelican Books
Tourism

Sir George Young was born in 1941 and was educated at Eton College, where he won an Open Exhibition in Modern Languages to Christ Church, Oxford. After graduating in Politics, Philosophy and Economics he worked in a merchant bank in the City before joining the National Economic Development Office as an economist. His interest in tourism dates from his work as Kobler Research Fellow at the University of Surrey from 1967 to 1969; in 1970 he published *Accommodation Services in the U.K., 1970–1980*, which analysed the determinants of demand for accommodation away from home and projected demand forward to 1980. Since 1969 he has been Economic Adviser to the Post Office Corporation.

His interest in tourism has been practical as well as academic. He has represented the Greater London Council on the London Tourist Board and the London Convention Bureau, and has constantly pressed for a tourist plan for London. Sir George Young is married, with three children, and lives on the Thames at Cookham.

Tourism

Blessing or Blight?

George Young

Penguin Books

Penguin Books Ltd, Harmondsworth, Middlesex, England
Penguin Books Inc., 7110 Ambassador Road, Baltimore,
Maryland 21207, U.S.A.
Penguin Books Australia Ltd, Ringwood, Victoria, Australia

First published 1973

Made and printed in Great Britain by
Hazell Watson & Viney Ltd, Aylesbury, Bucks
Set in Monotype Times

Illustration designed by Mel Calman and Philip Thompson

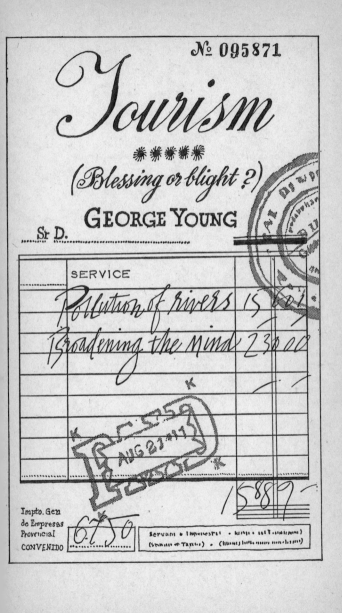

№ 095871

Tourism

✳✳✳✳✳✳

(Blessing or blight?)

GEORGE YOUNG

Sr D. ....

	SERVICE		
	Pollution of rivers	15	
	Broadening the mind	230 00	
		15 88	

Impto. Gen
de Empresas
Provencial
CONVENIDO

AUG 27 1971

67 50

Contents

Acknowledgements

I would like to thank the many people who helped me write this book; firstly, Jill Norman of Penguin Books, and Peter Hall, Professor of Geography at the University of Reading. Without their advice and encouragement, this book would have been neither started nor completed.

Secondly, Michael Pillans, who helped with some of the statistical work and with writing some sections of the book.

Thirdly, those who commented on the book in draft form. Professor Medlik and Dr Richards, both of the University of Surrey's Hotel and Catering Management Dept – to which I am also indebted for permission to draw on material from the thesis I did there as Kobler Research Fellow. Mr Fitzpatrick, now Director of Development and Traffic Commissioner at the Greater London Council and Mr Rogers, of the Director General's Department. Mr Janata, Senior Lecturer at the School of Hotelkeeping and Catering, Ealing Technical College and Mervyn Bryn Jones, formerly Charles Forte Research Fellow at the University of Surrey. To all these I am grateful for their helpful comments and suggestions. Any errors which remain are of course my own responsibility.

Finally, my thanks to my typist, Nina Porebska, for typing and re-typing this book either from illegible scrawl on paper or from unintelligible comments on tape.

George Young. November 1972.

1 Introduction

There are yet some other petty things which seem to have reference to this balance of which the said officers of His Majesty's Customs can take no notice to bring them into the account; as mainly, the expenses of travellers – *Thomas Mun, 1620*.

In the three hundred and fifty years which have elapsed since Thomas Mun wrote *England's Treasure by Foreign Trade*, tourism has grown from a minor fiscal nuisance to an industry of major social and economic significance. Many countries could not begin to balance their international accounts without those 'petty things' he referred to, totalling as they did about £8 billion in 1972 over the world as a whole.

In view of this volume of expenditure and its rate of growth, the importance of tourism is gradually being recognized and, in many countries, particularly the developing ones, it now warrants a Ministry all to itself. On a personal level as well as a national level, the significance of tourism is a matter for comment by the man in the street; the growing popularity of holidays abroad has brought him into direct contact with the tourist industry and, if he lives in a country which is a popular tourist destination, he will increasingly have found himself on the receiving end.

In spite of this growing awareness of the importance of tourism, many questions concerning it are not so much unanswered as unasked; and implicit assumptions which may have been valid twenty years ago are neither challenged nor substantiated. Does tourist expenditure really filter through to and benefit the local economy; or has the emergence of international airlines, international hotel companies, international travel agents and international banks meant that the benefits of tourist expenditure are now being siphoned away and reverting to the tourist's country of origin rather than his destination? Is it the case that the taxpayer or ratepayer of the tourist destination is in fact subsidizing the tourist – who is probably better off – by paying through taxes and rates for expensive tourist infrastructure and capital grants for hotels, without receiving adequate benefit? Is the traditional machinery of local government, geared to the priorities and requirements of local residents, able to control or plan for an ever-increasing influx of visitors from abroad? To what extent is the sustained and costly effort made by tourist authorities on behalf of many historic cities to attract and accommodate more tourists undermining their very appeal as tourist destinations? If there are saturation levels beyond which further growth in tourist arrivals brings more problems than rewards, what is being done to calculate those levels and see that they are not exceeded?

On a national level, is it really in the best interests of developing countries to graduate from an agricultural economy to a service economy based on tourism without the intermediate stage of a manufacturing economy? Might the effort of diverting a country's labour force into the tourist industry – where productivity gains are difficult to achieve – impede growth rather than accelerate it?

On an international level, does the machinery exist to control and coordinate this essentially international phenomenon? And what will happen when the populations of India and China achieve sufficient disposable incomes to afford holidays abroad?

When looking for the answers to some of these questions it becomes clear that attitudes to tourism, on a personal as well as a national level, are almost consistently contradictory. On a personal level, popular opinion is in favour of removing certain restrictive trade practices which have the effect of keeping the cost of inclusive tours and of air travel artificially high and which thereby inhibit the growth of international tourism. Yet popular opinion is as strongly opposed to the increased noise and traffic at airports – and indeed to new airports themselves – which would necessarily follow the abolition of those practices. Again, on a personal level, there is a reaction against the increasing uniformity which is manifesting itself at tourist destinations, where, regardless of country, the tourist stays in identical hotels, hires identical cars and watches identical American films on television. Yet the same tourist is the first to complain if his own language is not spoken, if the standards of comfort to which he is accustomed at home are not met or if the native diet is alien to his digestion. On a national level, grants and loans were introduced to assist the hotel industry in the UK and to encourage tourism, at the same time as the industry was severely penalized by the introduction of the Selective Employment Tax. The Greater London Council gives £85,000 annually to the London Tourist Board to assist the promotion of tourism to London at the same time as it states that a continued increase in visitors is totally unacceptable. A new airport is justified at Maplin on the basis of traffic estimates far in excess of the region's capacity to absorb visitors after they have landed. Concorde is developed at great expense by one government department, while another makes its commercial success doubtful by introducing new legislation on noise.

It seems therefore that there is a need for a more coherent, logical and up-to-date approach to tourism, both at the personal and national level. Its role in a given country needs to be more clearly identified so that the benefits of tourism can be encouraged and the pitfalls anticipated and circumvented. The consequences of continued growth must be analysed; and if found to be unfavourable, then attitudes must change. Freedom to travel should no longer be viewed as an absolute good, to be pursued at all costs, but as a relative good to be restrained when it prejudices other more important goals. Failure by the tourist industry to change its historic attitude will result in it attracting a backlash not unlike that occasioned by urban motorway proposals, when sections of the public believe that the price society is paying for greater mobility is too high.

The layman or the legislator who wishes to inform himself on the subject and find the appropriate solution for his own circumstances is hampered by the paucity of suitable literature. Tourism is an untidy industry, which sprawls inconsiderately over a number of industrial classifications and academic disciplines, and this has undoubtedly impeded the development of a good bibliography. The literature tends to cover selected component parts of tourism rather than the phenomenon as a whole. There are books on the structure and growth of the hotel and catering industry; (there are apparently seven books on the Savoy Hotel alone); on the emergence of the British seaside resorts; on the development of holidays with pay; on the history of air travel; on the international conference industry; and on a host of other subjects – such as the history of English inn-signs – which are peripheral to the central theme of tourism.

Of the few contributions which have been made on this central theme, too high a proportion are written from entrenched positions with predictable lines of fire. Those who represent the airline industry are forever complaining of a shortage of hotel beds – because they are unable to sell seats on their aircraft unless their passengers are assured of accommodation at their destinations. On the other hand, those who represent the hotel industry are constantly complaining of an excess of accommodation – because the more beds there are, the lower their occupancy rates and the greater their difficulty in raising tariffs. Tourist authorities insist that if their promotional budgets and staff were cut, tourist arrivals to their country would slump; on the other hand, the econometricians maintain that tourist arrivals in a given country are related to the level of air-fares and the average incomes in the tourist generating countries – and that the impact of advertising is at best marginal and at worst a complete waste of money. Airport authorities insist that newer and larger airports are urgently needed if international air traffic is not to grind to a halt. On the other hand, conservationists argue that existing airport capacity is ample if only the authorities concerned would arrange their affairs more efficiently. The cynic will argue that the growth of international travel is destroying primitive cultures and corrupting the few remaining unsullied places on earth with decadent Western values. The idealist will respond that international travel has a unique role to play in breaking down the prejudices and misunderstandings that all too often lead to war. The sociologists, inevitably, disagree amongst themselves as to what the future holds. On the one hand it is argued that the world is becoming more homogeneous, and therefore the diversity of possible experiences is being gradually eliminated. Since this is the very stimulus to travel, it is argued, travel will eventually become pointless. On the other hand, it is said that man is a restless, nomadic creature and his basic instinct to explore will never be snuffed out. For those in pursuit of the truth about tourism, it is a confusing journey littered with false trails. When confronted with a signpost, the safest thing to do is to ask who put it there, before too much credence is placed on its message.

This book is an attempt to describe tourism, to identify what the important issues are and to indicate where the solutions might lie. It is not aimed at the experts in the field of tourism, but at the man in the street; for it is he who, in the final analysis, should make the vital decisions about the role that tourism should play in the life of his country. Unless he has some basic knowledge of the tourist phenomenon, there is a danger that these decisions will be pre-empted by those with interests which may not be those of the country. With a better understanding of the key issues, the man in the street may be able to question long-held beliefs about the tourist industry and to change outdated attitudes. As the controversial issues mainly concern the growth of international travel as a leisure pursuit – rather than in the course of business – it is this side of tourism which is examined most fully. However, business travel and domestic tourism are also included where relevant.

To meet these broad objectives, the book is partly descriptive – showing how tourism has grown and describing in fairly broad terms the nature of the tourist phenomenon – partly analytic, looking at the underlying trends, the structure of the industry, the way governments deal with it – and partly admonitory, looking at the lessons which can be learnt from the mistakes of others and at the solutions which appear to be most favourable.

After this introduction, the book is divided into seven chapters, each dealing with one broad aspect of tourism. Chapter 2 is mainly descriptive and recounts the history and growth of tourism, primarily as it concerns the UK. As with so many other modern phenomena it transpires that annual holidays, seaside resorts, and even centrally-heated hotels can be traced back to the ancient Romans. This chapter looks briefly at developments since then, and provides the background to the other chapters which are mainly concerned with issues of today and of the future.

Chapter 3 examines the tourist himself and the many influences on his behaviour. Who is he, and what is it that motivates him to travel? What makes him decide where to go, how to get there and what to do when he arrives? It tries to identify the nature of the relationship between factors such as income, social class and age and the propensity to travel, and from this draws some conclusions on whether the large increases in tourist traffic currently in evidence are temporary phenomena or the beginning of a sustained and apparently indefinite period of growth. It also looks briefly at the business traveller and the conference delegate.

Chapter 4 describes, in broad terms, the tourist phenomenon. How many international tourists are there and how fast are their numbers increasing? Where do they come from and where do they go to? How much do they spend, where do they stay? The chapter suggests that current methods of measuring tourism, which concentrate on numbers and dollars spent, are inadequate in that they do not measure the demographic or social impact of tourism, and it puts forward new types of measurements. The chapter ends with a brief description of the tourist phenomena in the UK and its concentration in London.

Moving on from the incidence of tourism, Chapter 5 looks at the structure of the tourist industry which has grown up in response to this demand. It examines the trends towards vertical and horizontal integration within the industry, particularly in the UK, and identifies the problems which have emerged through the different components of the industry expanding at incompatible rates.

Chapter 6 looks at the impact which the various aspects of tourism mentioned in the two previous chapters have on the tourist destinations within the countries concerned, and pays special attention to those cities and areas – particularly London – which are the most popular tourist destinations and where problems of conflict clearly arise. It sees how these localities benefit or suffer from tourism; it looks at the impact of tourism on the local residents, on town planning, on employment patterns, on traffic and on the responsibilities of local government, and identifies areas of conflict between tourist and resident. It also examines the less obvious conflict between national government and local government on matters related to tourist policy, and puts forward suggestions for tilting the balance in favour of local or regional government when tourist policy is being formulated.

Chapter 7 moves further up the tourist infrastructure and looks at tourism from a national, as opposed to a regional and local point of view. It looks at the arguments which have convinced governments to subsidize the tourist industry and questions some of them. It tries to assess the impact of tourism on the growth of the economy as a whole and looks at the way different administrations react to, control or encourage tourism. Particular attention is paid to the analysis of problems which arise when tourism grows too fast, and the Caribbean Islands are examined in this context. Because tourism is basically concerned with people, the social considerations and effects – which are all too often ignored – are explored. Where attitudes are changing on the benefits of tourism, attention is paid to the reasons for those changes, and to the solutions which are being adopted by the more far-sighted administrations. Efforts to channel the dynamism of tourism in beneficial directions receive especial attention.

The last chapter is of necessity speculative as it is concerned with the future. Every industry has the prophet of doom among its commentators; we are told that computers are going to reduce individuals to numbers; that the effluents from chemical plants are going to poison our drinking water; that town planners are going to make us live in square boxes in vertical streets; that the power industry is going to melt the North Pole and drown us; and, of course, that the politicians are going to blow us to pieces.

Tourism is not short of its own peculiar prophets; the green fields of Europe will shortly be covered with airports; the air will be filled with the noise of jets flying in jumbo-loads of tourists; our capitals will be submerged in a sea of new hotels; the roads congested with tourist coaches; historic buildings even more cluttered with culture-seeking visitors; streets populated with souvenir shops, boutiques and strip clubs. Already the phrase 'pollution by tourist' has been coined.

This final chapter draws together the arguments from the preceding chapters and on that basis has a look at the future. It looks at existing forecasts and forecasting techniques, and sees how previous forecasts have come unstuck. Where it appears that problems are going to arise, it suggests remedies for anticipating and avoiding them.

In a book of this nature and length it is difficult to do full justice to the subject of tourism; if aspects of it are excluded or dealt with superficially it is because they are not the ones which need cause the reader concern. If the balance of the argument appears against the tourist industry, this is partly to remedy the bias of existing literature and propaganda which overestimates its value, partly because the book has concentrated on the worrying aspects where further thought and research is urgently needed, and partly because it looks at tourism from the host's point of view rather than the guest's.

2 History of Tourism

Like many other modern industries, tourism can trace its ancestry back to the Old Testament. Whereas nowadays travelling for pleasure exceeds travelling for business, there can be little doubt that in those days business trips predominated, particularly if one included military campaigns under that heading. Chapters xxvi and xxvii of the Book of Ezekiel describe trade and commerce in ancient Tyre and recount the travels abroad made by the merchants. Perhaps the first tourist in the modern sense was the Queen of Sheba, who paid a special visit to King Solomon in Jerusalem out of curiosity.[1] For those lower down the social scale, there was relatively little opportunity for travel; the generous provision of holidays – mainly religious ones – afforded the time, but the absence of good communications, the paucity of disposable incomes and the danger involved acted as important deterrents.

In Ancient Greece, mobility began to increase; when the first Olympic Games were held in 776 BC, it is recorded that visitors came to Mount Olympus from all over Europe and the Middle East. In the fourth century BC, Xenophon recommended that public money should be spent on building hotels for visitors to Athens, a policy which, twenty-five centuries later, gained acceptance in Western Europe.

If part of the pattern of modern tourism can be traced back to Ancient Greece with crowds at the Olympic Games and State support for the accommodation industry, another part can equally be traced back to the Ancient Romans. The sheer size of the Roman Empire and the associated problems of administering it called for an efficient network of roads connecting the capital to the various outposts. These roads were built primarily for the administrative and military sections of the population, but, once built, they provided the ordinary citizen with the means and opportunity for travel. This pattern of a breakthrough in travel being provided by the public sector – in particular the military sector – and then being exploited by the private sector is now a familiar one, exemplified by the development of the jet, and V-TOL aircraft. Travelling in the Roman Empire was safe and convenient to a degree unknown again until the beginning of the nineteenth century. The traveller could leave Hadrian's wall in the north and travel the 4,500 miles to Ethiopia on first-class roads. By using relays of horses, it was also possible to cover long distances in short periods of time; Caesar travelled from the Rhone to Rome in eight days, while the fastest journey is commonly attributed to Tiberius who travelled the 200 miles from Tichinum to Drusus in 24 hours.

As with later manifestations of tourism, it was business travel which led to the routes, and indeed to the hotels being constructed, later to be exploited by travellers for pleasure. Because the hotels which the Romans built, unlike the roads, no longer exist, it is forgotten that the development of the two was complementary. The reasons which were later to motivate the stage-coach companies, the railways and the airlines to invest in hotels also required the Romans to build them to get the best return from their investment in roads. Their hotels, or posting-houses, stood on the main roads, usually in a town or village. In between, at distances of six miles, were mutations, which were basically stables where horses could be changed – the equivalent of today's petrol stations. Lanciani has described the remains of a Roman hotel excavated in the Great St Bernard. 'The Roman hospice . . . comprised a temple to the God of the mountain, a hospice for travellers, stables and watering troughs, and storehouses for fuel and provisions. The hospice was built in stone with an elaborate system of hypocausts and flues for the distribution of heat throughout the guest-rooms.' – a comfort still absent in many of today's hotels. Some of these hotels could only be used by officials with a *diploma tractatorium*, carried by those on official business, a custom still observed with VIP lounges at some airports.

The Roman citizens benefited from these roads and travelled on them frequently in the summer months. At that time of year, there was a general exodus from the cities to the coast, while the richer Romans went abroad for their holidays, some to commit the sacrilege of scratching their names on the pyramids. The banks of the river between Canobus and Alexandria teemed with luxury hotels frequented by Romans and foreigners alike. Friedlander tells us that 'all the shore from Toscana to Terracina and from Terracina to Naples and round the gulf up to Salerno was lined with marble palaces, baths, gymnasia, temples, a wealth of Roman splendour.' The situation is much the same today, and the water-based summer holiday in Italy has a very long history.

With the decline of the Roman Empire in the fifth century AD, the conditions in which tourism could flourish on this scale also disappeared. The volume of trade contracted and with it travel on business. The surfaces of the roads deteriorated and the roads themselves became infested with bandits; 'There is definite proof that from the decline of Rome until the middle of the last century, there was not much foreign travel.'[2]

The student of tourism can skip the millennium following the decline of the Roman Empire with equanimity. Apart from the pilgrims and the crusaders, whose motives were rather special, available sources indicate that tourism and travel were on a much reduced scale. Developments which are important in relation to the development of tourism today can be traced back to Elizabethan England and the emergence of the holiday away from home.

When Elizabeth came to the throne in 1558, there was a limited amount of travel on the highways in England; lawyers and their clerks were following judges on their circuits, students were travelling to and from the universities, merchants were seeking new outlets for their wares, and young men were travelling to London to make their names and fortunes. Before the Dissolution of the Monasteries in 1539, many travellers would have taken advantage of the free monastic hospitality, readily available in most parts of the country. Indeed, there were several monastic orders whose main function was the provision of accommodation for pilgrims and travellers; other orders established separate dormitories and refectories for travellers, and appointed certain monks to look after the guests. In 1539, 608 religious houses were suppressed by Act of Parliament and travellers were diverted elsewhere. Many would have gone to stay with friends and relatives instead. The rules of hospitality were less tightly drawn in those days, requiring neither notice in advance nor close ties of friendship for a guest to be made welcome. Indeed the extent of free hospitality was an important reason for the late development of commercial accommodation.

Travellers at that time differed in important respects from today's tourist;

There were virtually none who were travelling, like the modern tourist, because they loved travel for its own sake, or, like the visitor to the modern holiday resort, who took to strange places for rest and recreation. That people should come to do these things involved two important innovations; a change of mental attitude, and the coming into existence of places which were attractive to and made provision for the accommodation and entertainment of pleasure seekers. The first was unlikely to occur in advance of the latter, and the latter might seem to presuppose the former.[3]

It is worth noting that in 1618, a Royal Proclamation laid down definite closing times for ale-houses, after which food and drink might not be served to anyone other than a *bona fide* traveller; an Act which 350 years later still exists almost intact and which puzzles and annoys the overseas visitor to Britain – not to mention a large number of residents. Many of these ale-houses were to be found on the main lines of communication from London to the provinces, and it has been suggested[4] that these had been built to replace the facilities previously supplied by the monasteries. Accommodation off the beaten track, a fair description of roads at the time, was probably harder to find.

Tourism as we now know it owes its beginnings in no small way to the conviction held by the medical profession at the end of the nineteenth century that mineral water contained ingredients beneficial to the human constitution. In 1562, Dr William Turner published a *Book of the Natures and Properties as well as the Bathes in England and of other Bathes in Germany and Italy very necessary for all sick persons that can not be healed without the help of natural bathes.* In his book, Dr Turner puts forward a remedy: 'There are manye in the north and northwest partes of England, and some in the Easte partes, whyche beynge diseased with sore diseases would gladlye come to the bath of Baeth.' Dr Turner's influence on his colleagues and their influence on the leaders of society were such that the waters of Bath became nationally famous and encouraged the discovery of other springs elsewhere, notably at Tunbridge Wells and at Epsom.

The transition from visiting these resorts for reasons of health as opposed to reasons of pleasure was a slow one, lasting for many centuries; the transition from inland resorts to seaside ones was slightly quicker; the final transition, from resorts inside the UK to resorts overseas is still taking place, but has been even quicker still. There is therefore a logical chain linking the excursions to the watering places in medieval England to today's annual trips to the Spanish shores.

Dr Turner's book provides incidental ammunition for those who maintain that the tourist facilities provided in the UK fall short of those provided on the continent.

He that had been in Italye and Germanye and had sene how costly and well-favouredly the bathes are trimmed and appoynted there in divers and sundry places, woulde be ashamed that anye straunger whyche has sene the bathes in foren landes should look upon oure bathes. For he woulde thinke that the straunger woulde accuse us Englishmen of three thinges; of grosnes and brutish ignorance because we cannot trim our bathes no better; of unkindnes because we do so lightly regard so high and excellente giftes of Allmighty God; of bestlye filthiness because we make no partition between ye men and ye women whilse they are in bathing but suffer them contrary both unto the law of God and man to go together lyke unreasonable beastes to the destruction of both bodye and soull of very manye.

The seasonality of tourism also provoked suggestions at that time. In a book published in 1631, *A Discourse on Natural Bathes*, Dr Jordan suggested that 'our Queen's bath and Crosse baths, being small baths, were covered,' adding 'that it would be no harme to this City if it be a meanes of procuring more resort hither in the wintertime, or more early in the Spring, or more late at the Falle.'

The transition from visiting the resorts for health reasons to visiting them for pleasure had begun by the Civil War, and astonished men like Goldsmith. 'To a person who does not thus calmly trace things to their source, nothing will appear more strange than how the healthy could ever consent to follow the sick to those places of spleen, and live with those whose diseases are ever apt to create a gloom in the spectator.' But the spas offered the only escape from London, and as they became more consumer-oriented, offering amusements, entertainment and better accommodation, so people of wealth and fashion gravitated towards them, even though they were in good health.

Ancillary trades were quick to notice the commercial implications arising from the discovery of new springs; the success of the better known spas demonstrated to landowners, shopkeepers, innkeepers and physicians that the establishment of a spa within their catchment area could have beneficial multiplier effects. Today's competition and tension between rival resorts can be traced back to a broadsheet issued in 1684 entitled 'An exclamation from Tunbridge and Epsom against the new found wells at Islington'.

Interlopers are abroad, and we must cry out as the Quack Doctors doe – Beware of Counterfeits for they swarm; could not folkes be content to invent new fashions and new oaths, new religions and new models of government, but the divil must put them upon to find out new wells, and new physical waters, when there were old ones enough of all conscience to have scoured their gutts and purged their purses and make work for the doctors... Audacious and Unconscionable Islington. Was it not enough that thou hast... been the metropolitan mart of cakes, custards and stew'd pruans, the chief place of entertainment for suburb bawds and loitering apprentices? Famous for bottled ale... could not all these advantages satisfie thee without invading our privileges, trumping up your spouts and old dormant holes to intercept our customers?

The seventeenth century also brought with it the stage-coach, which facilitated travel enormously. It is not certain whether the coach that left Chester for London on 9 April 1657 was the first one, but the method of travel which it introduced remained popular for two centuries. Accommodation sprung up along the routes of the stage-coaches, bringing custom and prosperity to the favoured villages.

Travel and tourism in those days were for the few; life in the seventeenth- and eighteenth-century watering-places resembled in many ways life on a cruise or in a small winter sports hotel, where the company is small and self-contained, rather than the modern seaside resort, where the individual is submerged in the crowd. Richard Nash, Master of Ceremonies at Bath, was able to welcome each visitor personally, but a social life as exclusive as this could not survive the intrusion of outsiders in any numbers. As travel and tourism filtered down the social scale in the eighteenth century, the watering-places gradually changed into holiday resorts. Already by the beginning of that century, the position of the traditional watering-places was being challenged by small seaside fishing villages, decaying harbours and deserted heaths which attracted the followers of the new sport of sea-bathing. It had been discovered that many of the mineral wells at the spas contained not a trace of minerals, and so the patrons concluded that the advantages of bathing could be obtained more conveniently and economically from the sea. Those who bathed in the sea did so naked. Conclusive evidence of this can be found in an engraving in the British Museum by John Setterington of Scarborough Bay in 1735. This transition from inland to the coast transformed many small agricultural communities, with some fishing industry, into holiday resorts. Brighton was being visited by holiday-makers in 1730, and by 1786 Blackpool was emerging as a popular resort.

The truth was that the advantages of the inland watering places over their 'adversaries' was superficial, and the deficiencies of the seaside resorts could be easily remedied. Adequate for the needs of a privileged minority, and reflecting in the highly organised and confined social life the tastes of this narrow section, the spas depended for their prosperity on the monopoly of a limited number of mineral springs, and they were inadequate to meet the rising demand which resulted from the expansion of trade and industry. The capacity of the seaside resorts, on the other hand, was unbounded. While social life at the spas was necessarily focused on the pump-room and the baths, and there was no satisfactory alternative to living in public, the sea coast was large enough to absorb all comers and social homogeneity mattered less.[5]

Thus it was that the increasing volume of tourism changed its pattern, as the resources which were appropriate for a smaller number could no longer cope.

The final transition from the tourism of those days to the

phenomenon that we know today was marked by the growth in international travel. Contemporaneous with the growth of the spa was the growth, on an infinitely smaller scale, of travel abroad by Englishmen. The motivation, however, was different; Justus Lipsius (1547–1606) wrote 'Of old and nowadays, great men have always travelled. But the use of any sensible voyage was increased knowledge of manners and customs and constitutions of foreign lands, and a broadening of the mind.' – as opposed to a healing of the body. Two centuries later, we find from the writings of Volney, *Travels through Syria and Egypt*, in the 1780s that the motives were broadly unchanged.

I had acquired a taste, and even a passion for knowledge, and the accession to my fortune appeared to be fresh means of gratifying my inclination, and opening a new way to improvement. I have read, and heard repeated, that of all methods of adorning the mind and forming the judgment, travelling is the most efficacious.

Arthur Young, who visited France in each of the years 1787–9, had as his object 'to ascertain the state of cultivation, wealth, resources and natural prosperity of the Kingdom of France, which survey he undertook for the benefit of his own country.'

Student travel was also an eighteenth-century phenomenon. Adam Smith noted, in 1776, that 'in England it becomes every day more and more the custom to send young people to travel in foreign countries immediately upon leaving school and without sending them to any university. Our young people, it is generally said, return home much improved by their travels.'

If pleasure was not perhaps the main motive behind foreign travel – as it is now – its pursuit was not abandoned when the destination was reached. In his book *Travels*, written in the early eighteenth century, Keysler records that

... though most young travellers are apt to give a loose to their propensities to pleasure, even in Italy; yet the English may be said to run greater lengths than the others; for having a great deal of money to lavish away, it not only gives them more spirit to engage in adventures, but likewise furnishes them with means of removing impediments, or buying off any ill consequences.

It is not surprising that, in some cases, the end product of the grand tour was a source of disappointment to the sponsor. Adam Smith recalls that

... in the course of his travels, he generally acquires some knowledge of one or two foreign languages; a knowledge which, however, is seldom sufficient to enable him either to speak or write them with propriety. In other respects, he commonly returns home more conceited, more unprincipled, more dissipated and more incapable of any serious application either to study or to business, than he could have well become in so short a time had he lived at home. By travelling so very young, by spending in the most frivolous dissipation the most precious years of his life, at a distance from the inspection and control of his parents and relations, every useful habit which the earlier parts of his education might have had some tendency to form in him, instead of being riveted and confirmed, is almost necessarily either weakened or effaced.

The advantages, or disadvantages, of travel overseas were, however, only for the few. Almost as important as the motives were the deterrents; travelling abroad, right up to the middle of the last century, was both expensive and dangerous. Local tolls and taxes, coupled with unreliable rates of exchange for foreign currency, meant that the traveller had to take with him adequate resources to cope with all eventualities – such as a prolonged stay in hospital due to strange diseases. The gold he often had to take made him easy prey for highwaymen. Under these conditions, prerequisites for travel overseas were wealth and courage – assets which are not always found together.

By the beginning of the nineteenth century, many of the characteristics of modern tourism were discernible, and developments during the century were destined to add considerably to the volume of traffic – both within the country and to the continent. This was due to the after effects of the Industrial Revolution, which had five important consequences for tourism.

Firstly, it shifted the centre of gravity of the workplace away from the agricultural countryside to the industrial conurbation. This was ultimately to lead to a demand for periodic escape back to freer, quieter and more salubrious surroundings. It is now a well-established fact that town-dwellers are more intensive users of recreational facilities than country-dwellers, and this locational change was to be an important stimulus to tourism.

Secondly, in addition to changing the locality of the workplace, the Industrial Revolution changed the nature of the work done. The seasonal variety and leisurely progress of agricultural life was replaced by the relentless monotony of factory routine. This was to add to the urgency for holidays and for a relief from the strain.

Thirdly, the growing power of the trade unions and the increased commitment of the government to social legislation was eventually to lead to the granting of annual holidays with pay. This took a hundred years to achieve.

Fourthly, the Industrial Revolution generated wealth which did not accrue to the aristocratic landowners but to the middle-class industrialists, and ultimately to their employees. This was to add significantly to the numbers of those who could afford to travel.

Finally, the invention of steam locomotion brought mobility to people on a scale and at a price hitherto undreamt of. In 1816, the first crossing of the Channel by steamboat took place, and the first regular service began in 1820. By 1840, 100,000 people were crossing the Channel each year. By 1882, the figure had increased to 500,000 and by 1902 it had doubled to one million. Proposals to construct a channel tunnel, so topical today, occupied transport authorities in the nineteenth century. The original idea is popularly attributed to Napoleon, who conceived it as a method of invading England. It was resuscitated periodically throughout the century, and received serious attention from the Select Committee on the Channel Tunnel in 1883. Details of the tunnel, as it was then planned, were given to the Committee by Sir Edward W. Watkin, Bt MP, Chairman of the South Eastern Railways Company and Hon. Chairman of the Submarine Continental Railway:

> The popular idea of a tunnel is a hole which is very dark and damp and which is very much like the bottomless pit; the tunnel which is the subject of our efforts would be a place under the sea as light as day, lighted by the electric light, lined so as to look pleasant and agreeable, perfectly ventilated and capable of carrying a maximum of traffic under the circumstances that attend such a tunnel.

On the possible cost of such a tunnel, Sir Edward said 'I have myself taken a round figure and I say that £3 million ought to do the tunnel itself.' Current estimates are in the region of £500 million. Sir Edward's trains would have travelled at an average speed of 45 mph and their capacity would have been 14 million passengers per year, and 30 million tons of goods.

An exchange between the Marquis of Lansdowne, Chairman of the Select Committee, and Sir Edward, revealed that some elementary demand analysis had been carried out to justify the proposed investment. Marquis of Lansdowne: 'Are you under the impression that you could offer very great attraction to the public . . . and might I ask whether those attractions would be in the manner of cheapness of travelling?' Sir Edward: 'I think so, for this reason, that wherever you find a large traffic, you also find a tendency to reduce prices . . . it pays better to carry full trains at a low price than it does to carry half-empty trains at a higher price.' (This neatly summarizes the current problems of the scheduled airlines *vis-à-vis* their chartered competitors.) Another remark of Sir Edward's is of relevance today in the context of the possible loss of American traffic through insufficient airport capacity; Sir Edward said 'There is no doubt that if there is to be no tunnel, traffic will more and more go direct to the continent and less and less through England to the continent.'

While the growth of traffic to and from the continent by boat was important, it was of course steam locomotion and the development of the railways which had a major impact on travel. Once the fear and unfamiliarity of rail travel had been overcome, there were few practical restrictions on travel between any two major towns. This initial fear was well described by Dr Granville in 1841.

It has been alleged that the being wafted through the air at the rate of twenty or thirty miles an hour must affect delicate lungs and asthmatic people; that to such as are of sanguineous constitution and labour under fulness of blood in the head, the movement of rail trains will produce apoplexy; that the sudden plunging into the darkness of a tunnel and the emerging out of it as suddenly cannot fail to make work for the oculists; and finally it had never been doubted but that the air of such tunnels is of a vitiated kind and must give rise to the worst effects; while that at the bottom of deep cuttings or excavations, being necessarily damp, will occasion catarrh.

The same sorts of misgivings were doubtless expressed about air travel a hundred years later, and will probably be expressed about space travel. History shows that such fears can safely be discounted.

The following table shows how the railways grew in the middle of the nineteenth century:

	1835	1845	1855	1865	1875
Total mileage opened					
GB & N. Ireland	471	3277	13411	21382	16803
Total passenger miles (m)					
GB & N. Ireland	23	51	79	160	604

The initial impact of the railways was to increase short day-trips; the normal fifteen minute service between London and Greenwich had to be trebled at Whitsun and Easter. Excursion trains, probably invented by Sir Rowland Hill, were more fully developed by Thomas Cook, the architect of modern tourism. His first publicly advertised excursion was from Leicester to a temperance demonstration in Loughborough on 5 July 1841. The return fare was one shilling and 570 people went. From these relatively modest beginnings, Thomas Cook went on to build an organization which has been a household word in travel ever since. In 1855, Cook started his first continental operations by marketing travel to the Paris Exhibition, and this can be said to mark the beginning of the inclusive tour. By having contacts and travel bureaux in every country, by having favourable arrangements with hotels, shipping companies and railways all over the world, Cook could offer the customer at the counter an itinerary which would have taken him weeks to organize, as well as costing him a good deal more.

But in the nineteenth century, the availability of cheap and easy travel was not in itself enough; there was no tradition of travel amongst the new Victorian middle classes and there were formidable practical obstacles to surmount – such as the language problems, prejudice at home and overseas, exchange rates and, in due course, passports. The rich overcame these difficulties when travelling by employing guides and couriers, while the hotels in which they stayed at their destinations were familiar with their language and solicitous for their needs – and their money. The new tourists of the mid Victorian age – the bank clerks, the solicitors' wives – could not afford these services, yet desperately needed the assistance they provided. Thomas Cook had the foresight to recognize these problems, and the organization to solve them. 'He deliberately set out to be a universal courier, doing for those who could not provide themselves with courier's services what the courier did for those who could afford to hire him.'[6] The excursion from Leicester to Paris in 1855, where the all-in cost of four days in Paris, including accommodation and return ticket was 36/-, was described in the *Manchester Guardian* as 'an event in the history of railway travel'.[7] It did, in fact, mark the beginning of the inclusive tour abroad.

The influence of Cook in the field of travel cannot be over-emphasized. His originality lay in his methods, his almost infinite capacity for taking trouble, his acute sense of the needs of his clients, his power of invention and his bold imagination which made him the greatest of all travel agents. He invented the now universal coupon system, and, by 1864, more than a million passengers had passed through his hands. It is interesting to note that in 1880 he organized a package tour to the Passion Play at Oberammergau.

If the railways, Victorian prosperity and Thomas Cook provided the means for tourism, the growth of annual holidays was to provide the opportunity. At the beginning of the nineteenth century, the country was predominantly rural, the rhythm of life was leisurely, and sufficient respite from work was afforded by the traditional holidays related to the great religious feasts, local fairs and times of year when the pace of agricultural life was slow. And being a predominantly rural community, there was of course ready access to the open countryside for leisure activities.

By the end of the century however the country had become predominantly industrial, and pressure from the unions and the more enlightened MPs had made a start towards giving the average employee an annual holiday. Such pressure was resisted by the employers, and a typical employer's view on the subject can be found in the evidence given to the Select Committee on Child Employment in 1843 by a Staffordshire China manufacturer.

As a manufacturer, I have not the least doubt but that I should prosper greatly if I could depend upon the working powers of men. They often come about the premises, but will not buckle to. If I give them a day or two at Easter, they take a week; if at Christmas, they take a week; indeed, they are not to be depended on.

More enlightened employers, prodded by liberal reformers such as Lord Shaftesbury, started giving annual holidays and by the second half of the nineteenth century, weekly half-holidays in industry became more common. The Bank Holiday Act of 1871 gave statutory sanction to some of the traditional holidays and indeed added to them. Referring to the Act, *The Times* commented 'There has been an increasing tendency of late years among all classes for holidays. Among those that are well-to-do, the annual trip to the seaside has become a necessity, of which their fathers, or at least their grandfathers, never dreamt.' This shows how one generation's luxury becomes the necessity of the next.

By the 1890s the Royal Commission on Labour showed that most people had a weekly half-holiday. At the end of the century, as the quality of the social legislation improved and wage levels rose, the lengthy transition from weekly half-holidays to longer annual holidays began. By the outbreak of the First World War, workers at Rowntree's factories were enjoying two weeks paid holiday.

There was a subtle social distinction of the type only found in Britain between that section of the working population that spent a fortnight at the seaside resort and the other section that had to be content with a day's outing to Blackpool or Southend. For in the same way as the middle classes had joined the aristocracy at the eighteenth-century seaside resorts, so did the working classes join them there in the nineteenth. By then the aristocracy were graduating to holidays overseas where they were, again, pursued firstly by the middle and ultimately by the working class.

The increased volume of travel generated hotel building; hotels existed in name in the eighteenth century, but tended to consist of sets of self-contained apartments rented out for relatively long periods. In the nineteenth century, the railway companies built hotels at their termini but London, though acknowledged as the capital city of the world, lagged behind America and the rest of Europe, in particular Switzerland, in standards of hotels. This was rectified in August 1889 when the Savoy was opened by D'Oyly Carte, with W. S. Gilbert and A. Sullivan as the principal shareholders. The Savoy claimed to be the best hotel in the world and boasted seventy bathrooms. The only comparable London hotel – the Victoria, which opened two years earlier – had four. D'Oyly Carte had pioneered the use of electric light in the Savoy Theatre and naturally installed it in his hotel. The prospectus informed the visitor that

. . . the only artificial light used over the entire building will be electric light, and the supply will be continuous during the hours of day and night, not only in the sitting-rooms, but in bedrooms, the button or switch in the bedroom being so placed that the light can be turned on or off without getting out of bed. The electric current will be obtained from a large installation in the base of the hotel, so that the supply will not depend on any outside source.

This stoic independence from the London Electricity Board is still a feature of the Savoy's electricity supply – a feature for which its patrons have frequent occasion to be thankful.

Apart from London, most of the hotels were on the coast. There was still implicit faith in the therapeutic qualities of the sea and this was reflected in the names of the seaside hotels – such as the Hydropath. By the end of the century the more sophisticated and market-oriented of the resorts had started to use sunshine statistics for advertising purposes. The Isle of Man had a Tourist Board before the First World War, and its TT (Tourist Trophy) Motorcycle Race must have been one of the first deliberately created tourist attractions.

Throughout the nineteenth century and right up to the outbreak of the First World War, travel abroad, and travel to the UK by foreigners, proceeded apace. The period of peace which followed the Napoleonic Wars and the development of the railways reduced the physical hazards of travel, and Thomas Cook removed the administrative ones. In 1840, Dr Arnold could write 'In fact Switzerland is to England what Cumberland and Westmoreland are to Lancashire, a general summer touring place.'

By the outbreak of the war, the tourist movement had developed from a local phenomenon to a world phenomenon, from which countries such as Austria, France, Italy and Switzerland were deriving substantial incomes. The factors behind this growth were various and the influence of education as a motivational force was probably stronger then than it is now. 'Curiosity about strange places and strange lands, and a taste for novelty and change. It was education that mattered most – an educated interest in the customs and manners of other nations and it was amongst the most earnest of the middle and working classes that continental travel first found a foothold.'[8] There were already signs of the great American invasion which is such a feature of twentieth century tourism. It was estimated by shipping companies that before the First World War, 150,000 Americans crossed the Atlantic annually to Europe where their expenditure was reported to be gratifyingly extravagant.[9] The Americans were also responsible, in part, for the growth of the conference; in 1831, on his return from a visit to the United States, De Tocqueville wrote 'Americans of all ages, and of all classes and of all tendencies, are forever forming associations.' By 1909, the Union of International Associations estimates that over 100 international conferences were being held each year.[10]

As the world drifted into the darkness of the Great War, the pattern of tourism was beginning to resemble the pattern that we know today; people with time and money went abroad; people with less time and money went to the seaside; people with no time and money stayed at home. Further, as the population of a country grew richer, so it adopted the holiday-taking patterns of the privileged few.

The First World War stimulated research and development on the aeroplane; this is a good example of a military breakthrough being subsequently exploited for civilian use. Improvements in both speed and safety in the twenties ensured ultimate success after some inconspicuous starts. The first fare-paying scheduled trip between London and Paris took place on 25 August 1919. There was one passenger – a reporter from the *Evening Standard* – and the journey took $2\frac{1}{2}$ hours in a De Havilland DH4A owned by Aircraft Transport and Travel Ltd. It was not a success, and within nineteen months all scheduled services were abandoned – including those which had recently commenced between London, Brussels, Amsterdam and Cologne. The average number of fare-paying passengers per trip was only $1\frac{3}{4}$. Fear and the absence of avatories – a fatal combination – were the major deterrents. In the early days of air travel services were irregular and aircraft were cramped and noisy to the point that conversation was impossible. Cabins were not pressurized and the passenger was subjected to a good deal of vibration; the cruise altitude of the aircraft meant a bumpy ride except in the best of weather. Nor was the price competitive; London to Paris by air was, initially, six times as expensive as by rail. By the late twenties, larger and safer planes had made flying more attractive and by 1939, there were regular flights between London and all major European capitals.

Another feature of the inter-war years was the growth of the holiday camp. Their development is quite rightly associated with the name of Sir William Butlin, although several charitable bodies had already started to provide camps for the poorer sections of the community before he founded his first holiday camp in 1936 at Skegness. Constructed at a cost of £100,000 it could hold 2,000 people, and was opened by the famous flying star Amy Johnson. It provided comprehensive facilities – arrangements for looking after children, free swimming lessons, and dancing – and exceeded in scope anything hitherto in operation. Visitors were drawn primarily from the small salaried class, not from manual workers.[11] Although not exorbitant by today's standards, the charges of £3 10s. per week were undoubtedly beyond the means of the average manual worker. Other organizations followed Butlin's lead. Thomas Cook opened a camp at Prestatyn in 1939 and two camps were planned by Travco Ltd, although one was not completed. By 1939 it was estimated that there were well over 100 camps round the coast with a total capacity of 30,000 per week.

Inland, development of hotels took place in the cities. In London, the Park Lane, Mayfair, Grosvenor House, Dorchester and Strand Palace Hotels were all built between 1927 and 1932. As these were bad years for the British economy, the hotel industry must clearly have been assisted by the lavish spending of overseas visitors – at any rate in London. In 1925, the Maharajah of Patila reserved the whole of the fifth floor of the Savoy, comprising some thirty-seven suites. A silver bath was installed and a special kitchen built for the chef and his retinue of fifty to prepare curries and native delicacies.[12]

Holiday camps and hotels were assisted by the extension of holidays with pay and by a growing official recognition of the importance of tourism. Yet even then some of the danger signals – analysed in later chapters – were visible, particularly in Europe. In 1925, Aldous Huxley wrote that 'Forty miles of Mediterranean coast have been turned into one vast pleasure resort . . . one vast shuffling suburb – the suburb of all Europe and the two Americas – punctuated here and there with urban nuclei.'[13]

Within the UK, the growth of tourism was seen, in some quarters, as a similar threat. This is shown in the Report of the Departmental Committee on Deer Forests.[14] The Committee had been asked, among other things, 'How far the productive use of these lands is compatible with their continued use for any, and if so what, sporting or recreation purposes?' They reported as follows:

The owners [of the deer forests] had no practical means of excluding strangers, even if they wished to do so, owing to the time and expense of taking out an interdict against every separate person. The value of certain forests adjacent to tourist centres is considerably depreciated by the frequency of disturbances during the stalking season.

The concept of the dual use of land had not developed very far. Throughout the 1930s, committees, economists and academics started looking at the tourist industry. In 1936, A. Norval, Professor of Commerce and Industrial Economics at the University of Pretoria, wrote,

It [tourism] is of very great national importance and constitutes one of the major credit items in the international balance of payments of the UK. That the tourist industry has not been developed to the same extent in the UK as it has been developed in several of the continental countries must, in the main, be attributed to the laisser-faire policy which dominates the economic life of Great Britain and to the extreme British conservatism. While most of the Governments of the countries of the continents on both sides of the Atlantic are actively engaged in the development and promotion of their tourist traffic from other countries, the attitude of the responsible authorities of Great Britain appears to be one of extreme indifference.[15]

Another economist in the thirties, Robertson, in *The Control of Industry* was more constructive. 'It is even possible that the part ultimately reserved for the British Isles in the scheme of the inter-national division of labour will be that of a playground and park and museum to exercise the youth and soothe the declining years of the strenuous industrial leaders on either side of the Pacific Ocean.' Perhaps the most perceptive commentator on tourism at the time was F. W. Ogilvie.

The tourist movement has assumed such dimensions in the last decade that the great moving markets of tourists are now an important factor in many balances of payments in international trade, and the livelihood of whole towns and districts in many countries. The nation of shopkeepers is already in large measure a nation of innkeepers, but it knows little of it, mainly because of the many defects of our official passenger statistics.[16]

Forty years ago, Ogilvie identified two trends which have remained an important feature of tourism, though one might not describe them in his terms. The 'increased vulgarisation of traffic', and, following from this, the 'diminished length of average stay and diminished average expenditure in any one place or country'.

The growing interest in tourism by economists, geographers and even politicians – Lord Snowdon[17] and Neville Chamberlain[18] mentioned it frequently in speeches in the thirties – led to greater attention being paid to the statistics of tourism. This topic is still one which aggravates today's student of tourism, and clearly caused trouble between the wars.

While the ideal is to embrace national no less than international movement, the material for a study is everywhere defective at present, and in most countries almost non-existent. . . If the principal tourist countries of the world agreed to collect their statistics in roughly the same form, they would have the rare satisfaction of solving the statistical problems for themselves and for others at one and the same time.[19]

The UK was a notoriously bad offender in this respect; in 1927, the International Statistical Institute addressed an inquiry to thirty-two countries about their tourist data. The Chairman of this project noted that nearly every country either already had the required data or was taking active steps to procure it. But 'pour ce qui regarde la Grande Bretagne, de telles statistiques vont au dela des developpements probables.'[20] Ogilvie pinpointed the trouble remorselessly. 'The British Board of Trade apparently regards this part of its task as so very delicate indeed that, year after year, it has shirked it altogether.'[21]

Other countries woke up to the significance of tourism long before the UK. In the 1930s, the Swiss Government knew what types of hotels tourists from different countries patronized – a detail still not known in the UK. In 1929 both Canada and the US carried out sample surveys of tourists travelling overseas but 'what the Departments of Commerce in the US and Canada had done, and done successfully, for five years, could the British Board of Trade not even try to do?'[22]

The outbreak of the Second World War put an end to domestic and international tourism; during the war, many hotels were requisitioned and used for other purposes; others were bombed. But the war accelerated the development of the aeroplane and the construction of airfields, and this was to prove more important, in the long term, than the loss of hotels. The war also forced many people to take an active interest in foreign countries and this added to the travel motive when hostilities ended.

During the war, many far-sighted plans were drawn up in the UK for implementation when peace came. Many had to do with leisure, and they were praiseworthy as far as they went. If they were deficient, it was because they underestimated the demand for the motor-car and overestimated the growth in home-based, as opposed to overseas holidays.

Between 1950 and 1956, tourist traffic to and from member countries of OECD (Organisation for Economic Co-operation and Development) grew at levels of between 10 and 16 per cent per annum; between 1956 and 1960 this growth rate stabilized at a level of between 6 and 10 per cent, and during the 1960s it rose again to 10 per cent.

Tourist arrivals in the UK rose from 200,000 in 1946 to 1·7 million in 1960; and to 7·2 million in 1971. Revenue over the same period increased from £12 million in 1946 to £170 million in 1960; and to £491 million in 1971. Traffic to Spain increased even more dramatically – from 4 million in 1959 to 24 million in 1970. During these two decades, air travel eclipsed sea travel and in 1957 the number of air passengers crossing the Atlantic exceeded the number of sea passengers. The fortunes of BEA alone demonstrate the growth of air transport; in 1946, BEA served eleven destinations in Europe. In 1972 it served ninety-one. Over the same period, the number of passengers carried increased from ½ million to 9 million, and the type of plane progressed from Viking, Elizabethan, Viscount, Vanguard, Comet to Trident.

While most of the growth was provided by people entering the holiday market for the first time with one annual holiday abroad, the icing on top of the cake was provided by people taking a second holiday in winter; the number of winter package holidays sold in the UK alone rose from 6,900 in 1963–4 to 600,000 in 1971–2.

The rest of the book deals with the post-war situation in more detail; if one lesson emerges from the study of the history of tourism, it is that it is not a 'flash in the pan' – a form of consumers' expenditure which is here today and gone tomorrow. It has deep roots in the history of man, and as modern conditions – large increases in per capita incomes, more stable political conditions and extensions of paid holidays – remove the barriers to tourism, so the pent-up volume of energy is released. And without these barriers – or new ones – so will it continue.

3 The Tourist

Who is a tourist? This raises firstly the problem of definition. Broadly speaking, a tourist is someone who travels away from home, and in this book the definition is not restricted to those who travel for pleasure. Having accepted this broad definition, it is then convenient to divide tourists into three distinct categories; those travelling for pleasure, those travelling on business and those travelling to attend a conference. The motivations and growth rates for each category are different; so are their travel patterns and spending habits. For this reason they are dealt with separately.

Travelling for pleasure

This is the largest section of the international market, and the fastest growing. In broad terms, the reasons for this growth are rising income levels in Western Europe and North America, and longer paid holiday entitlements. While these are the principal reasons, there are many other subsidiary ones which are in some way related – rising levels of terminal education, increased levels of car ownership, greater social mobility and the concentration of the labour force into non-manual jobs. Arthur D. Little, a firm of consultants, have produced the following table which shows the relationship between some socio-economic factors and the propensity to travel.[1]

Factor	Influence on Travel
Income	Positively related
Education of head of household	Positively related
Occupation of head of household	Positively related to status
Paid vacation	Positively related
Urbanization	Negatively related

Age of head of household	Negatively related
Life cycle	Negatively related to child impedance and age
Race	Non-whites less active
Sex	Males more active

It is in fact easier to analyse the deterrents to travel than the motivations, and to see to what extent these deterrents are likely to be removed in the future.

Basically, old age, the presence of small children, the absence of sufficient paid holiday and a shortage of disposable income are the traditional deterrents. While the latter two factors will, over a period of time, gradually diminish in importance, the first two will always be deterrents to some extent, particularly for long trips. The following table taken from a British National Travel Survey[2] shows the relationship between age and tourism.

Relationship between Age and Propensity
to take a holiday lasting four nights
or more away from home

Age	Percentage of age group taking a holiday
16–20	62
21–24	56
25–29	56
30–34	60
35–44	61
45–49	55
50–54	60
55–64	58
65+	42
All age groups	55·5

Part of the reason why older people travel less is probably a concealed income effect – they also happen to be poorer. However, research in America has isolated the effect of age on its own and proved that old age is in itself a deterrent to travel. Again, this may not be due to old age as such but to the physical disabilities which accompany it. If this is the case, then medical advancement, coupled with a reduction in the average age of retirement, could mean that in the next thirty years there will be increased demand for international travel from older people. There is a further reason for believing this to be so; today's older people grew up in an age where there was no tradition of frequent international travel and it never became part of their life style. Research by the Outdoor Recreation Resources Review Commission supports the existence of this familiarity effect. 'The survey suggests that wide-spread experience with outdoor recreation now will mean that in future older people will have higher participation rates than those of today.'[3]

If older people are currently below average as far as propensity to travel is concerned, younger people are above average. The following table shows the high percentage of total non-business visits made to the UK in 1970 which were accounted for by the 16–24 age group.[4]

Total number of visits and visits by young people from European Countries, 1970

Country of permanent residence	Total non-business visits to Britain	Percentage of non-business visits made by 16–24s	Number of non-business visits made by 16–24s
Belgium	240,000	40	96,000
Finland	20,000	39	8,000
France	530,000	32	170,000
W. Germany	520,000	31	140,000
Holland	300,000	30	90,000
Italy	170,000	26	45,000
Norway	40,000	45	18,000
Portugal	20,000	30	6,000
Spain	70,000	30	23,000
Sweden	120,000	33	40,000
Switzerland	130,000	32	42,000

Many of this age group are still continuing their formal education, so vacations provide them with the opportunity to travel on a scale denied to their less fortunate contemporaries who have taken up full-time employment. Being neither married, encumbered with children, mortgages or hire purchase commitments, they are free to travel for these reasons as well.

Young people are also able to travel more cheaply. Their resistance to the discomforts of life, their ability to hitch-hike and sleep rough mean that the premium for entering the travel market is

ower for them than for others. There are however two trends
ulling in opposite directions. Any trend towards earlier mar-
iages and earlier family formation will remove young people from
he travel market, whereas any trend towards a higher proportion
f school-leavers continuing their education beyond the compul-
ory school-leaving age will keep others in.

If the tourist is likely to be young rather than old, he is also likely
o be rich rather than poor; and this relationship between higher
ncomes and demand for travel poses one of the greatest challenges
hat modern society has to face. The extent to which shortage of
isposable income is currently deterring travel is shown by the
ttached table.[5]

Relationship between income and non holiday-making

ncome	Percentage not taking a holiday away from home lasting four nights or more
Under £450	67
£450–649	70
£650–749	56
£750–949	52
£950–1199	45
£1200–1449	33
£1450–£1699	27
£1700–£1949	30
£1950–£2499	22
£2500+	15

67 per cent of the lowest income group take no holiday away from
home, whereas the percentage of the highest income group is only
15. The table therefore gives some idea of the demand which might
be released as the lower income groups graduate to higher income
levels and adopt the same behaviour.

Studies of the nature of this relationship between income and
demand[6] suggest that a family spends very little on travel while it
s acquiring the basic necessities of life, but once this plateau is
reached, expenditure on travel increases quite fast. The British
National Travel Survey shows[7] that this plateau effect occurs
round about £1,200 per annum in household income. The important
factor for world tourism is the calculation of these various plateau

levels for the highly-populated, but currently poor, Asian, South American and South African countries. It may well be a long time before the Chinese take to mass tourism, but the scale of the problem for transport and accommodation is such that it should not be ignored.

The following table sheds some light on this issue. It is an index of passenger mobility in 1961 compiled by taking an average of the following measurements for the countries concerned: passenger miles per capita, passenger cars per capita, rail lines per 100 square miles, rail lines per 10,000 population, surfaced highways per 100 square miles, and surfaced highways per 10,000 population.[8] It shows the wide gap in mobility between developing and the developed countries and indicates the potential for future mobility.

Index of passenger mobility of selected countries in 1961

Index of France = 100

Developing countries

2–5	5–10	10–15	15–20	Over 20
Ethiopia	UAR	Peru	Algeria	Ceylon (22)
Nigeria	Burma	Paraguay	Malaya	Mexico (23)
Iran	Ghana	India	Brazil	Chile (36)
	Philippines		Bolivia	
	Syria			
	Thailand			
	Ecuador			
	Colombia			
	Indonesia			
	Pakistan			

Developed Countries

40–60	60–80	90–100	Over 100
Japan	Netherlands	France	USA (147)
Italy	Norway	UK	Canada (149)
	Finland	West Germany	
	Austria		

The income threshold at which expenditure on tourism begins varies from country to country. It has been suggested[9] that for American families the level is $10,000 (family income), and that for Europeans it is significantly less. The average for the world as a whole is probably somewhere between $500 and $1000 per capita.

Perhaps as important as the level at which tourist expenditure commences is the rate at which it subsequently increases. This income elasticity coefficient has been estimated by the Foreign and Commonwealth Office to be 1·5 and by IUOTO (The International Union of Official Travel Organizations) to be 1·88.[10] (This means that for each 1 per cent increase in income, expenditure on travel rises by 1·9 per cent). Figures for individual countries have also been calculated by IUOTO. The figure for France is 3·2, for UK 1·6, and for West Germany 1·8. Given continued growth in personal incomes, expenditure on travel is likely to continue at a proportionately faster rate. This is important when the implications of continuous growth in demand come to be considered.

The table indicates another matter of interest. A very high income is not a guarantee that its recipient will in fact travel. 15 per cent of those earning above £2,500 stayed at home. There is therefore a form of 'leakage' at the top end of the market. The homes of the very rich may be such that they have no reason to 'escape' from them. Indeed, as the congestion at their traditional watering-places increases, so there is added incentive to stay at home. The same pattern is observable in America where a significant percentage of the richest section of the community (earning over $10,000) either take a holiday at home (9 per cent), or take no holiday at all (19 per cent).[11]

The effect of income on second holidays is even more marked than it is on main holidays and is shown in the following table.[12]

Relationship between income and taking an additional holiday away from home, lasting four nights or more

Income	Percentage of GB holiday-makers taking an additional holiday
Under £450	14
£450–649	14
£650–749	4
£750–849	8
£850–949	10
£950–£1,199	9
£1,200–£1,449	14
£1,450–£1,699	15
£1,700–£1,949	25
£1,950–£2,499	25
£2,500+	25
All	14

Families with pre-tax incomes of over £1,700 are nearly twice as likely to take an additional holiday as the average family. This is undoubtedly an area of expansion with tremendous implications for the tourist industry, particularly that section of the industry geared to winter holidays.

In addition to being younger and richer, the average tourist enjoys a longer than average entitlement to paid holidays and, as holidays with pay become more and more generous, so an important barrier to future growth will be lowered. In spite of considerable progress in extension of paid holidays since the war, the UK still lags behind many European countries in this respect.[13] Entry into the EEC should narrow this differential. Most European countries already have statutory three-week holidays for all workers, and some have higher minimum levels. European countries also have more public holidays than the UK; there are currently six public holidays in the UK and no other country in the world has fewer. Most have considerably more; for example, Italy has eighteen and West Germany fifteen, although some countries like Lesotho, which celebrates National Tree Planting Day and Malawi which celebrates Mother's Day, clearly are less scrupulous about the pretexts for public holidays than the UK.

Length of paid holiday is important in two ways. First, it influences initial entry into the tourist market and second, any increase affects the behaviour of the tourist once in the market. Surveys carried out by the British Tourist Authority[14] and ORRRC[15] have shown that the longer the holiday entitlement the more likely that a holiday away from home will be taken. Where the head of the family was allowed any form of paid holiday, 52 per cent of heads of families and wives actually travelled away from home. By contrast, of those entitled to paid holidays of four weeks or more, 64 per cent travelled away from home.

Both American and UK figures show that where the length of paid holiday is two weeks or less, this puts a ceiling on the length of vacation away from home which is seldom exceeded. However, as the paid holiday entitlement lengthens, there is a tendency for two or more holidays to be taken instead of one. A University of Glasgow Survey says

Generally speaking, the longer the total holiday from work in the year, the less the tendency to use it all up during the current trip. It may be expected therefore that as annual holidays with pay increase in length, the tendency towards secondary holidays will also increase.[16]

These second holidays tend, not surprisingly, to be shorter than main ones, to be based on the weekend rather than mid week, and more likely to be taken in the months of September and May than in any others. This wide distribution of second holidays is in marked contrast to main holidays, which are heavily concentrated in the months of July and August, and lengthening of paid holidays can therefore bring with it a better seasonal distribution for the tourist industry.

Life-cycle stage is another important determinant of tourist demand. As regards entry into the tourist market, British data are unfortunately limited but the annual British National Travel Surveys[17] do show that households with infants up to the age of four are less likely than the average household with children to take a holiday away from home. At the other end of the spectrum, the single adult under forty-five[18] is most likely to take a holiday away from home. The lower participation in holidays by households with infants is predictable, as infants clearly require special facilities which are not readily available away from home. The absence of small children increases the likelihood that a holiday will be taken for another reason; the wife is more likely to be earning and this will reduce some of the financial obstacles to holiday-taking. The Vacation Travel Attitude Survey[19] gives an interesting insight into parental attitudes where holidays with children are concerned. 55 per cent of those interviewed actually thought a vacation was more fun for the parents when shared with the children. A further 32 per cent were less enthusiastic, but dutifully paid tribute to the idea that children ought to be part of the holiday. 11 per cent looked upon a holiday as a welcome relief from the tedium of looking after children. The same survey showed that those who are married or single are equally likely to take a holiday away from home, but the widowed or divorced are less likely to do so.

In considering the influence of different occupations and levels of education on the tourist, it is difficult to isolate these effects both from each other and from the income effect, because the more attractive occupations, higher terminal levels of education and higher salaries all go hand in hand. However, U K statistics[20] indicate that the non-manual worker is almost twice as likely to take a holiday away from home as the manual worker. Amongst manual workers, the skilled are more likely to take a holiday than the unskilled, although there is almost certainly an income effect at work here. Even at the top of the occupational tree – a category comprising directors, managers and proprietors – 22 per cent do not take a holiday away from home; this shows that there are barriers which neither high incomes nor secure and successful jobs can break down. It is interesting to note that the worker paid by the week is less likely to take a holiday than the worker paid by the month.[21] This cannot be attributed to differences in income as available data show that the former's average earnings are in fact higher than the latter's.[22] This may be due to the greater incidence of holidays with pay available to the monthly-paid worker. Similarly, although there are no income differences to explain the phenomenon, shop assistants and clerical staff are much more likely to take a holiday than the average worker in manufacturing industry.

The low-level of holiday-taking of the unskilled is also found in other European countries,[23] and there is obviously an enormous untapped source of future demand here, if and when the barriers of income, lack of education and paid holiday are removed. The same effect may however be achieved in time through changes in the pattern of employment involving a transfer of labour from traditional heavy industries to service industries.

The individual's occupation also affects to some extent the timing of his holiday. A government Social Survey[24] shows that 50 per cent of unskilled workers take their holiday in July while only 20 per cent of professional and intermediate workers do so.

The final major determinant of tourist behaviour is the terminal level of education. It has already been seen that in the eighteenth and nineteenth centuries, tourism was the prerequisite of the rich and well-educated. It was thought at that time that no education was complete without the 'grand tour'. Although the pursuit of knowledge *per se* is no longer so important a motive, a high level of education is undoubtedly helpful in overcoming fears and pre-judices, and in enabling the individual to acclimatize himself to new surroundings. The Vacation Travel Attitude Survey[25] showed that the college graduate in the USA was very interested in trips to Europe which included sightseeing – particularly to England and France – and that he concentrated on places of historic interest. He showed little interest in spending his vacation at an American resort hotel, which was much more popular with the non-graduate. The effect of education in the UK can be clearly seen by the fact that only 47 per cent of those who leave school at the minimum age take an annual holiday, whereas 70 per cent of graduates do so.[26]

What is important about all these determinants of tourist demand is that they are increasing, and increasing fairly rapidly. Income levels, education levels, paid holiday entitlements, occupation levels are all rising and as they rise so demand for tourism and the number of tourists increase. This must be the answer to those who claim that the present increases in tourist flows are straws in the wind. Research in many countries has shown the close and lasting relationship between the socio-economic characteristics mentioned above and the desire to travel, and there are no reasons whatsoever for believing that this relationship is going to break down in the next decades.

The previous paragraphs assume that the individual wants to travel, but no analysis of the tourist would be complete without mentioning motivation. Having discovered what sort of people travel, it is now pertinent to ask why they wish to do so. It is a subject which has occupied psychologists and sociologists for some time, but many of their conclusions are somewhat nebulous.

The modern tourist is characterised by his retreat into a shell; he is driven by permanent restlessness; he escapes into pleasure and he does not begin to know anything by himself.[27]

Anyone concerned with the motivation of travel has to realise first that he is reaching deep into one of the major conflicts of the human mind: a desire for sameness, the return to the womb, if you wish; conflicting with the motivation to reach out and discover the world. In a sublimated fashion, a trip is therefore a form of birth or rebirth.[28]

Motivation for tourism has been analysed somewhat more intelligibly by the Westflanders Development Council. They concluded that there were six principal reasons for man wishing to travel. 1. The need to escape from daily trouble and lack of freedom. 2. The need to show one's affection for other members of the family. 3. The need to maintain social contacts. 4. The need to show one's importance to other people. 5. The need to convince oneself of one's own achievements. 6. The need to keep oneself active and healthy for the future.

Research in the USA indicates that the wish to travel – as distinct from the ability to travel – is fairly widespread. Lansing and Blood discovered from their surveys[29] that only 17 per cent of people who did not travel gave as their reason 'respondent or other member of the family does not like to travel'. Studies by Travel Research International[30] support these findings. To the informal question 'Now we'd like to know how you feel about vacation travel in general, rather than about any one trip; please pick the sentence on this card that best describes you.' Only 3 per cent chose 'I really don't like to go away on vacation, but I go along for the sake of others in the family.' And only 1 per cent chose 'I don't like to travel on vacation and I manage not to.'

The major deterrents to travel are not motivational but practical; and as the practical limitations are removed in the ways outlined earlier, so tourist flows will increase. The point is well made by a further survey by Lansing and Blood,[31] the results of which are reproduced below.

Reasons why Americans don't travel

Reasons given	%
Too expensive	62
Cannot leave business or job	18
Lack time, too busy (due to non-business activities)	7
Too busy (for either business or non-business reason)	6
Respondent or other member of the family does not like to travel	17
Children or other dependants	12
Health	7
Too old	2
Other	9
Total (some people gave more than one reason)	140

Perhaps the best way of finding out why people travel is to ask them. As far as international travel is concerned, surveys of

tourists from various countries have been carried out to find out
the main reasons why they are travelling. The table below repro-
duces the results of one such survey[32] of Australian travellers to
Europe, both past and intending.

Reasons for Australians travelling overseas

	All travellers %	Past travellers %	Intending travellers %	Past visitors to Britain %	Intending visitors to Britain %
See different places/things	60	55	65	65	52
Broadening/ educational	43	41	45	48	36
See relatives/ friends	31	36	26	23	43
Exciting/ adventure/ pleasure	21	19	23	22	18
See different people	16	15	16	20	11
Re-visit homeland	13	14	11	10	18
See places heard about	10	15	6	12	8

Australians think that the most important reason for international travel is the chance it gives to see different places and
things. This is followed by the educational motive, and the wish
to visit friends and relatives. A further survey[33] carried out for
the BTA showed that the three main attractions for Americans
visiting the UK were the friendliness of people (31 per cent),
buildings with historic interest (30 per cent), and green and
beautiful scenery (23 per cent).

Looking more specifically at the reasons for coming to Britain,
these are shown in the following table.[34]

If these are the reasons why people come to the UK – and surveys of tourists from most other countries confirm this general
picture – then the popularity of Britain is not likely to diminish.
If it depended on more transient attractions – like Carnaby Street
– then the UK tourist industry could be more vulnerable to

The most attractive aspects of a visit to Britain (top ten)

	All travellers	Travellers choosing Britain first
	%	%
Beautiful/scenic country	43	47
History/historical places	36	46
Castles/historic buildings	22	22
Visiting friends/relatives	19	28
Royalty/palace/changing guard	18	12
General sight-seeing	16	13
People/friendly people	16	20
Atmosphere/way of life	15	15
Theatre/ballet etc.	12	17
Nightlife/casinos/pubs	9	11

changes in fashion. Unless there is large-scale demolition of historic buildings, despoliation of the countryside and a sinister change in the traditional British good humour, then the UK will remain near the top of the international tourist's shopping list.

Travelling on business

Business travel is motivated by very different considerations from those that motivate travelling for pleasure, and the business traveller is a totally different animal from the tourist. Although there are fewer of them, they travel more often, spend more money, do not concentrate their travel in the peak months, and tend to stay for shorter periods of time. They are of enormous importance to the tourist industry; in Zurich, for example, 64 per cent of total hotel visitor nights are accounted for by people travelling on business.[35] In the UK, it has been estimated[36] that domestic business demand for licensed hotels and motels accounts for over 25 per cent of total domestic demand and for particular hotels the percentage is higher. A pilot study for a guest registration system carried out by NOP Market Research Ltd in 1968 for a leading UK hotel company revealed that over a two-month period 75 per cent of all arrivals at four of the company's hotels were accounted for by businessmen. In America, the importance of the business market is shown by the following table.[37]

Hotel and motel occupancy in USA by purpose of visit

Purpose of Visit	% of Visitor Nights
Conference	10·6
Business	35·0
Mainly business, some pleasure	4·5
Personal business	1·6
Mainly pleasure, some business	4·6
Pleasure	42·2
Education and culture	1·5
Total	100

Industrial Market Research Ltd have identified seven factors which influence the volume of business travel.[38] 1. Level of business activity. 2. Trends in employment. 3. Trends in the location of industry. 4. Trends in the structure of industrial and commercial enterprises. 5. Trends in travel motivation. 6. Improvement in means of communication. 7. Rationalization of company organization.

On the basis of this, one can say that whether an individual is a business traveller or not depends on the nature of his employment and on his status or type of job within that employment. Travelling salesmen for example are estimated[39] to spend 1,000,000 nights per year in some sort of commercial accommodation in the UK. On the other hand, most of those involved in local government are unlikely to spend many nights away from home on business as the nature of their employment confines their work to the local authority area in which they operate.

A person's status within the firm is also important. Clearly a worker manning a production line, a shop steward or a typist are unlikely to travel on business whatever the goods and services being produced by the firm. The sales manager, managing director or those employed in the distribution and transport section are more likely to travel on business. A survey[40] of the Commercial Lodging Market carried out in the US broadly substantiates this hypothesis. Sales managers were 3·65 times as likely to stay in an hotel as the average American. In the UK, a study carried out by NOP Market Research Ltd showed that manual workers represented 2 per cent of business arrivals at hotels, while the executive and managerial category accounted for 19 per cent.

It is possible that, in the future numbers of business visits will be reduced by increased use of the Post Office's Confravision service; this allows groups of people in studios to take part in conferences by the use of ordinary telephone lines. However, it is even more likely that any reduction of travel which this may bring about will be more than outweighed by growth occasioned by the changing structure of business. Employment in manufacturing industry is declining, and employment in the service industry is increasing. Automation is replacing manual workers and increasing the numbers of supervisory and administrative employees. The tendency for large companies to increase their share of the market and various other factors are all placing more employees in jobs where travel is more likely.

As far as the business visitor from abroad is concerned, it is not

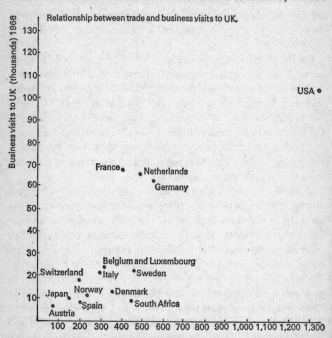

Figure 1.   Imports to, and exports from, UK (£ million)
Source: 1967 Annual Abstract of Statistics
Home Office Immigration Statistics

surprising to learn that those countries with whom the UK trades most also, broadly speaking, generate the most business traffic. Figure 1 shows the nature of this relationship. The United States, with whom our trade was greatest, supplied far and away the highest number of business visitors. More business arrivals from South Africa might have been expected in view of our considerable trade with that country, but the correlation between trade and business arrivals held good by and large.

In the future, there are likely to be more business travellers, and they are likely to make more visits. Continued growth in world trade, the expansion of domestic economies, the increase in numbers and influence of multi-national corporations together with the employment factors mentioned earlier all point in one direction; continued demands on the tourist industry to meet business needs.

Conferences

Conferences will increasingly become an important component of the economy. The trend nowadays towards the holding of meetings and conferences is not just a passing fashion, since the countless political, cultural and especially economic liaisons and unions demand repeated personal contact. This is why meetings and conferences are essential and will continue to be so. The tourist industry is particularly interested in conferences. . . It sees in them an additional market with a relatively high expenditure and a good seasonal distribution.[41]

The number of international conferences held in 1971 has been estimated[42] to be 5,000 attended by 3 million delegates. The value of this market is in the region of £400 million and it is growing fast.

It is therefore a dynamic part of the tourist industry and because there are signs that it is influencing the size and design of hotels, it deserves some attention. There are several reasons for the increase in the number of conferences and in the numbers of delegates attending them; perhaps most important is the increased specialization in many fields of commerce and professional activity and the tendency within those fields to pool knowledge, experience and research. One of the authorities in this field has identified other reasons.

The creation of many new independent states; the technical progress of means of communications; a larger understanding of the universal interdependence in economic, political and scientific matters; and a desire to solve such problems on a multilateral basis, to mention but a few. And among the results of this development are the creation of international organisations handling the problems mentioned above; the increase in international trade and travel, and much more. This development in itself, as well as the wish to foster it, has made an ever-increasing activity on the part of international organisations necessary in the form of international meetings of some kind – congresses, conferences, symposia, seminars and so on. The proliferation of international organisations and international congresses has again been further accentuated by two important trends in the post-war world, namely the specialisation within most fields of human activity – be it science, business, education or other topics – and regional co-operation in the form of political unions, custom unions, free trade areas, or other kinds of collaboration based on common culture, language or economic interests.[43]

Other factors are at work which will increase the size of the conference market; the availability of cheap group travel, the tendency to combine attendance at a conference with a holiday, and the growing influence and budgets of convention bureaux and professional conference organizers.

While international conferences can be of enormous assistance by securing a better year-round utilization of tourist infrastructure, they can cause problems if they are held in the peak of the tourist season. London was of course privileged to have played host to the American Bar Association in 1970; but it would be stupid to say that July was the most convenient month to have entertained 7,000 delegates and 3,000 wives. The growing importance of the conference delegate to the hotel industry manifests itself in the increased size of new hotels – although other factors are also at work. Conference organizers like to put all their delegates under one hotel roof for ease of booking and management. The hotels want to keep the high-spending delegate under that roof as long as possible, so tend to provide auditoria and other conference facilities, often free. Hence most new hotels are designed, where planning permission allows it, with 2,000 or more beds and with large rooms suitable for conferences.

Also of importance are domestic conferences; in the UK these comprise five main types. First, there is the social conference consisting of groups of people sharing a common leisure interest. These conferences are likely to grow with the reduction of the working week, increased length of paid holiday, rising standards of education, earlier retiring ages and increased life expectancy. Secondly, there is the professional and industrial conference whose popularity has grown with the increase of professionalism in business. A good example of this is the medical profession; as the practice of medicine becomes more complicated, so it is subdivided into many component parts; and the component parts are frequently subdivided further. This process has been accompanied by a corresponding growth in the professional associations representing the field of medicine, and the same principle applies to other professions, particularly in the fields of economics and sociology. This increased specialization has meant that it is more important for the people concerned to be in touch with research and other developments in their field of interest, and the conference is one of the main methods of securing this contact. Third, there is the sales conference, a profitable method of increasing sales of goods and services. Fourth, there is the Trade Association conference which can sometimes be very large indeed. For example, the Association of British Travel Agents had 1,500 delegates in 1968. Fifth, and finally is the political conference which can only be held at the larger resorts like Blackpool because of the volume of accommodation required and the necessity for a large conference centre where plenary sessions can be held.

Although London suffers from the lack of a purpose-built convention centre, it has proved a popular destination for both international and domestic conferences.[44] This is because conference delegates are looking for other features, principally easy accessibility, a wide range of accommodation, plentiful tourist attractions and an adequate supply of shops for their wives. (One third of international conference delegates are accompanied by their wives.)

Had the construction of the proposed convention centre in Covent Garden been proceeded with, London could have competed, in a very competitive market, on equal terms with other

European cities. This opportunity would, however, have brought with it problems; to be economic, the centre would have to be used frequently, and this would mean that the very large conferences, which now by-pass London, would have to come. This would add to the pressure on London's tourist infrastructure in the peak months, and this problem is further examined in Chapter 6. Careful management will be needed to ensure that any convention centre – if one is built – is used, where possible, in the off-peak months.

To sum up, the conference delegate, the business traveller and the ordinary tourist are going to want to travel more often and further afield. There will be more of them and their flows will be of increasing importance to national economies and to urban form. The next chapter looks at the tourist phenomenon in broader terms to examine these flows, and the following three chapters show their influence on the structure of the tourist industry and on local and national government.

4 The Tourist Phenomenon

International tourism is one of the fastest growing industries in the world, and is the largest single item in world trade; according to IUOTO, 181 million tourists spent $19·9 billion in 1971, excluding payments for international transportation.[1] 325 million tourist arrivals are forecast for 1980.[2]

This chapter seeks to describe, in general terms, the tourist phenomenon and to put it in perspective. It looks firstly at the world situation and then at that in the UK. In doing so, it uses a combination of four main methods of describing tourism. Firstly, tourism can be described in financial terms, quantifying tourist expenditure in destination countries. Secondly, tourism can be described in terms of movement, quantifying the numbers of arrivals at the frontiers of destination countries. Thirdly, tourism can be described by length of stay – quantifying the number of nights spent by visitors in destination countries. Fourthly, and here the chapter seeks to break new ground, tourism can be described in social terms, which enable one to measure the impact of tourism flows on the societies visited.

The first method, that of quantifying tourist expenditure, tends to be over-used; this is partly because it is one of the easier ways of measuring tourism, and partly because the reasons for promoting tourism are often closely connected with a concern for a healthy balance of payments. While the financial implications of tourism are of course important, and will be analysed in this and subsequent chapters, if tourism is viewed through financial spectacles alone then one's approach to it is necessarily a narrow one. That tourists may spend £1,500 million in London in 1980 is interesting, and encouraging for the balance of payments; that there may be 15 million of them is more interesting and potentially dangerous for the health of the capital. Because of a commercial approach to tourism, brought about by measuring it in terms of tourist pounds, too much attention is often paid to the advantages of growth in tourist expenditure, and too little to the disadvantages of growth in their movements and numbers.

The second method of measurement is essentially a measure of movement – how many visits are made to all the countries in the world each year? The problems involved in deriving this figure are explained later, but basically this method of enumeration has two defects; firstly it is not available for some countries; and secondly it measures visits, rather than visitors. If a tourist visits the same country twice, he is recorded as two separate visits; and if he visits more than one country, he is likewise logged more than once. The number of visits produced by this method is therefore higher than the number of visitors, and the gap may well widen with the growing popularity of second holidays, multi-destinational visits and international commuting by businessmen. For example, in 1971 Americans visited 2·8 countries per trip, as against 2 in 1965. However, the figure is a useful one as the number of visits is an important statistic for planners.

The third method is an elaboration of the second; instead of measuring the number of movements people make, it measures the number of nights they spend when they have arrived. It is therefore more accommodation based, and less transport based. By including length of stay, one derives a fuller picture than arrivals on their own can give, and since the latter are increasing and the former decreasing, use of both enumerators is really necessary to give an overall view.

The fourth method of measurement is hardly used at all at the moment but, if appropriate tourist policies are to be formulated and if planning for tourism is to be properly integrated with national planning, then this method of measurement needs wider recognition. It seeks to relate basic tourist statistics – as above – to social and economic factors in the host country. Thus, instead of simply stating the number of tourists, or the number of nights they spend, that number is expressed as a percentage of the number of residents, or of the number of resident-nights. Another example of using this approach would be to calculate tourist densities by expressing the number of tourists per square mile. Further, tourist expenditure as a percentage of total consumer expenditure is more meaningful than tourist expenditure on its own. Only by looking at the tourist phenomenon in this way, by calculating the ratios for countries of different size, population and economic development, can the impact of tourism be quantified and then compared.

Because of deficiencies in the world's tourist statistics, it is at this stage difficult to pursue this type of analysis very far. If, however, the thesis is eventually accepted that tourism has saturation levels beyond which it is inadvisable to expand, then concepts such as the ratio of tourist-nights to residents or of hotel beds to 'native' beds must be developed and used as they are more likely to indicate saturation points than simple numbers of tourist arrivals.

The tourist phenomenon is described in this chapter by a combination of all four methods described above.

Adding up the number of international visits is, in theory, very simple. However, some countries do not count tourists as they arrive and those that do do not have a common definition of a tourist. While the trend towards less formality at the frontiers is welcome from the traveller's point of view, it has deprived the statistician of his raw material; important tourist countries such as Austria, Germany, Belgium and Switzerland do not collect statistics of frontier arrivals. It is not therefore possible to present a reliable global total of frontier arrivals and, even if it were, such a figure would be of doubtful value as it would include day excursionists – who are not really tourists – and motorists who drive straight through a country without stopping. They are of little more relevance to a country's tourist industry than air-passengers who fly over without stopping. Ideally one should therefore deduct from frontier arrivals the numbers of such transient visitors and this consideration has led many countries to collect statistics of tourist arrivals at registered accommodation rather than at the frontiers. This figure must therefore be used, *faute de mieux*, where others are not available. Its use is by no means ideal as it excludes a large number of perfectly genuine tourists who are either staying with friends, or in accommodation which is not registered. (Some countries only register hotels.) A second defect of this method is that it leads to multiple recording of the same tourist. Each time he stays in a hotel in the same country he is counted, so the total number of visits recorded by this method is more than the total number of visitors staying in registered accommodation. One cannot therefore deduce how many tourists visit the country each year; and, if the number of visitors staying in registered accommodation increases, one does not know whether there are more tourists, or simply the same number moving about more.

The rather unsatisfactory situation that exists at the moment is therefore as follows. Some countries collect statistics of arrivals at the frontier and many of these distinguish between tourists – those who stay more than twenty-four hours – and day excursionists. Other countries collect statistics of arrivals at registered accommodation but there is no international agreement as to what accommodation should be registered; and, even if there were, it would exclude visits to friends and it would lead to multiple recording of mobile tourists. The figures of visits[3] which follow are therefore rather unreliable as they include different methods of quantification and definition.

Year	International tourist arrivals (millions)	Increase over previous year	Index
1950	25·3	—	100
1958	55·3	—	219
1959	63·0	13·9	249
1960	71·2	13·0	281
1961	75·3	5·8	298
1962	81·4	8·1	322
1963	93·0	14·3	368
1964	108·0	16·1	427
1965	115·5	6·9	457
1966	130·8	13·2	517
1967	139·5	6·7	551
1968	139·7	0·1	552
1969	154·1	10·3	609
1970	169·0	9·7	668
1971	181·0	7·1	715

Column 2 shows the annual increases, which have averaged nearly 10 per cent over the past ten years. Projected forward at the same rate to the end of the century, this would mean over 3,500

illion visits – a twenty-fold increase in thirty years. Clearly the
ourist boom has not yet begun, particularly since, in 1971, 95
er cent of the world's population did not cross an international
rontier.

The above figures exclude permanent migrants and those mov-
ng to seek employment. They also exclude domestic tourism
which probably represents between two thirds and three quarters
f total world tourist demand. In the USA, for example, over 350
illion trips are made away from home each year, many of which
would have crossed several international frontiers had they taken
lace in Europe.

Where do the tourists come from? The simplest way of answer-
ng this question is to divide the world into six regions and examine
he volume of tourism generated by each region. (The total is not
omparable with that of the previous table as the source is dif-
erent.)[4]

egion of tourist origin	International visits generated 1967 (millions)	%
urope	88·2	67·4
lorth America	37·3	28·6
atin America and Caribbean	1·1	·7
frica	1·2	·9
sia/Australia	2·1	1·6
liddle East	1·2	·8
otal	131·1	100%

75 per cent of all international tourist visits are in fact accounted
or by tourists from twelve countries – USA, Germany, France,
JK, Canada, Belgium, Netherlands, Italy, Switzerland, Sweden,
Denmark and Austria. 40 per cent of total tourist arrivals are
ccounted for by only two countries – USA and Germany – who
ave comfortably less than 10 per cent of the world's population.

These figures raise longer-term problems that will not call for a
olution until well into the next century; what will happen when
ncomes rise in the densely-populated but relatively poor areas of
he world such as India and China? Is there any reason for thinking
hat they will not behave as the inhabitants of the rest of the world
ow do, once their incomes have risen? If they do travel, where
vill they go? Answers to this can be found by looking at the
resent distribution of tourist visits.

The spread of destination countries is much wider than that of originating countries. The two most popular destination countries (Canada and Spain) account for about 25 per cent of the market, whereas the two most prolific suppliers of tourists account for about 40 per cent. International tourism therefore represents a dispersal, rather than a concentration, of people.[5]

Region of tourist destination	International arrivals 1971 (millions)	% of market
Europe	136·3	75·3
North America, Latin America and Caribbean	33·7	18·6
Africa	2·6	1·4
Asia/Australia	5·3	2·9
Middle East	3·4	1·8
Total	181·3	100·0

Europe is still by far the most important destination, with approximately three out of four international trips ending up there. To derive a picture of how tourism is changing, the 1971 figures are contrasted in the next table with those for 1950.[6]

Regional destination	1950 (millions)	% share of market	1971 (millions)	% share of market
Europe	16·8	66	136·3	75·3
North America, Latin America and Caribbean	7·5	30	33·7	18·6
Africa	·5	2	2·6	1·4
Asia/Australia	·2	1	5·3	2·9
Middle East	·2	1	3·4	1·8
Total	25·2	100	181·0	100·0

Although Europe increased its share of the market over the period, countries more remote from the principal tourist generating areas are now responsible for the fastest growth rates. The success of both Europe and the newer tourist regions further afield has been at the expense of the North American continent. Over the next two decades one might expect the four 'also-rans' in the above table to increase their share of the market at the expense of

Europe. This is because price is the single most important factor deterring travel to these areas. The airfare is the largest single component of that price, and airfares on these more remote routes are now coming down. On a cost per mile basis, New York–Tokyo is nearly twice as expensive at the moment as New York–London (5 cents against 2·9); over the next decade, this differential will narrow, and Europe's price advantage to North Americans will be eroded. A corollary of this is that air travel will continue to gain at the expense of surface travel, and that non-scheduled traffic will grow at the expense of scheduled traffic.

Tourist arrivals within Europe between 1950 and 1970 grew as follows:[7]

International tourist arrivals (thousands)

Destination Country	1950	1970	% increase
Austria	857	8,867	1,035
France	3,050	13,700	449
Greece	33	1,651	5,003
West Germany	1,026	7,715	752
Italy	3,500	14,189	405
Netherlands	368	2,399	652
Norway	534	1,049	196
Portugal	70	1,586	2,266
Spain	NA	24,105	NA
Switzerland	1,903	6,840	359
UK	618	6,730	1,089

Tourism is an expensive pastime; world expenditure on tourism, as derived from the IMF Balance of Payments Yearbook, was $15·3 billion in 1969 and since 1950 the percentage of world exports accounted for by tourism has doubled. Expenditure is not increasing as fast as numbers of visits, so average expenditure per visit is clearly falling. This is due to the operation of a number of factors; the development of inclusive tours – which effectively reduce the travel and accommodation costs of holidays; a trend towards visiting the cheaper countries – those with lower standards of living; and a decline in the length of visit due to the growth of multi-destinational visits and the faster growth of second holidays, which tend to be shorter than main ones.

Expenditure varies according to purpose of the visit; acting on the principle that one spends other people's money more enthusiastically than one spends one's own, it is natural that expenditure per day by business visitors is higher than those on holiday. (Indeed the fact that holiday visits are growing faster than business visits is one reason why average expenditure per visit is falling.) In the UK, for example, overseas visitors on business in 1970 spent twice as much per day as those on holiday. Because business visits tend to be shorter than holiday visits (7·1 days as against 12·8) expenditure per visit is in fact almost identical.

Daily expenditure by tourists varies according to their country of origin, but the relationship is not as simple as one might expect. Americans do not spend as much per day as tourists from a few obscure countries, not because Americans are poorer, but because the travel habit has filtered further down in America to the middle-income groups whereas in some Latin American countries with a less democratic sharing of wealth, travel abroad is the privilege of the very few and the very wealthy. With only 6 per cent of the world's population, the USA generates nearly one third of all international tourist expenditure.

Of the total expenditure of $15·3 billion in 1969, $9·1 billion was spent in Europe.[8] Principal beneficiaries in Europe that year were Italy ($1·6 billion), Spain ($1·3 billion), France ($1·1 billion), Germany ($915 million), UK ($862 million), Austria ($785 million) and Switzerland ($643 million). The biggest spenders were the Americans ($3·4 billion) and the Germans ($1·9 billion).[9]

On average, tourist receipts in OECD countries account for 6 per cent of total export earnings.[10] For Spain, however, the figure is 40 per cent, and for Austria, Greece, Ireland, Italy and Switzerland it is between 10 and 20 per cent.

All these tourists have to stay somewhere; many will stay with friends and relatives but OECD estimated that in Europe 254 million out of 569 million visitor nights are spent in hotels. There are probably over 10 million hotel beds in the world by now, though it is difficult to put an exact figure on this because of problems of definition and the poor quality of statistics.

The probable distribution of these hotel beds is shown in the following table for three years up to 1967.

Hotel and motel accommodation capacity (number of beds) % share

Region	1965	1966	1967	1965	1967
Europe	3,428,701	3,646,809	3,836,213	41·1	42·8
N. America	4,577,112	4,692,488	4,720,193	54·8	52·7
Rest of America	100,156	103,391	105,211	1·2	1·2
Africa	31,497	32,480	40,269	·4	·4
Asia/Australasia	157,956	174,934	203,274	1·9	2·3
Middle East	49,518	54,706	57,118	·6	·6
Total	8,344,940	8,704,808	8,962,278	100·0	100·0

The table shows that the percentage of hotel beds accounted for by the USA and Canada is falling; this is because domestic tourism is less buoyant than international tourism and the North American market is proportionately more dependent on domestic traffic than the other regions. Asia and Australasia are fast increasing their share of the market, confirming the trend seen in the previous tables on tourist movements.

In 1967, twelve countries had more than 100,000 beds each – Austria, France, Germany, Italy, Netherlands, Spain, Switzerland, UK, Yugoslavia, Canada, USA and Japan. In many countries, the average size of hotels is now over 100 rooms. These include countries such as Bulgaria, Hungary, Monaco, Portugal, Romania, Turkey, Puerto Rico, Philippines and Thailand. This list is not the same as the previous one; this is because it comprises the newer tourist destination countries, which are now building the larger hotels. The average size of hotel in the traditional tourist destination countries is lower because a large percentage of the hotel stock dates back to times when hotels were much smaller than they are today.

The argument introduced at the beginning of this chapter is now developed. To measure the social impact of tourism, it is clearly superficial to look at the sum total of arrivals. 12 million tourists in Switzerland are a different proposition to 12 million tourists in Australia. Ratios have therefore been calculated for a wide range of countries which show how many tourist nights are spent in a country per 100 residents. This provides an absolute measure of the demographic impact of tourism in a country, and a relative measure for the comparison of this impact between countries. The source of the table is I U O T O's annual publication of tourist statistics, supplemented by those of the O E C D Tourism Committee.

The table is interesting in so far as those countries which are typically associated with tourism – Spain and Italy, for example – do not come out at the top. This is the effect of relatively short lengths of stay, and of relatively large resident populations. The small islands in the West Indies produce the largest figures; anything over 36,500 would mean that, on average, there are as many tourists in a country as residents. There are no signs of any *countries* in the table reaching this figure in the near future, but it is undoubtedly the case that ratios for some of the tourist destinations *within* the countries are appreciably higher than those for countries as a whole. The figure for London is approaching 1,000; it is interesting to note that, using this measurement, the U K is more saturated with tourists than Spain, Italy, Yugoslavia and Jamaica. It is also interesting to note how high up the table countries like New Zealand and Lebanon are.

Later chapters of this book examine the impact of the tourist industry on those countries with very high figures, and demonstrate that diseconomies are beginning to creep in and to outweigh the advantages of tourism. For this reason, the progress of other countries – particularly those in Western Europe – should be monitored in case they start approaching these levels.

The second column measures density by calculating tourist nights per square mile; this ratio has been chosen rather than tourists per square mile in order to include lengths of stay. Sociologists are increasingly realizing the social effects of high density living, but the statistics they use exclude visitors. Again, these statistics need refinement so that the ratios for the areas *within* the countries can be derived.

There is a very wide range of densities – from Bermuda to Mali. The figure for London, which is an estimated one, is exceptionally high – and would have been even higher had it been calculated for inner London where the majority of tourists confine themselves.

Country	Tourist nights per 100 residents	Tourist density (Tourist nights per square mile per annum)	
Bermuda	3,249	78,918	
Bahamas	2,785	1,120	
Monaco	1,667	800,000	(H)
London	855	98,000	
Austria	798	1,846	
Malta	630	16,473	
Switzerland	333	1,312	(H)
Luxembourg	267	800	(H)
Lebanon	206	1,360	
New Zealand	181	49	
UK	172	1,026	
Spain	156	263	
Italy	127	529	
Israel	124	450	(H)
Jamaica	121	589	
Cyprus	117	200	(H)
Yugoslavia	105	228	
San Marino	105	869	(H)
Fiji	101	73	
Costa Rica	82	72	
Bulgaria	80	158	(H)
Hong Kong	74	7,306	
Belgium	71	585	
Denmark	71	206	(H)
Greece	69	120	
Tunisia	68	76	
France	66	157	(H)
Jordan	63	46	
Singapore	59	53,876	
Norway	56	17	(H)
Netherlands	47	451	(H)
Morocco	46	40	
Portugal	45	120	
Hungary	44	125	
Kuwait	35	33	
West Germany	28	171	
Libya	26	1	
Kenya	22	11	
Argentine	17	4	
Panama	14	6	
Syria	14	11	
UAR	14	5	
Iran	12	5	

Country	Tourist nights per 100 residents	Tourist density (Tourist nights per square mile per annum)
Uganda	8	8
Thailand	7	12
Colombia	5	2
Ceylon	4	16
Philippines	2	7
Tanzania	2	1
India	1	5
Pakistan	1	3
Malaysia	1	1
Ethiopia	1	1
Mali	·4	·05
Congo	·3	·4

(H denotes that only nights in hotels have been used in the calculation. The table should therefore be interpreted with caution.)

Another measurement which should be developed is that of hotel beds per 1,000 residents. This enables one to see the impact which the accommodation industry has made on a country, and approximate statistics have been derived for 1969.

Hotel Beds per 1,000 population

Belgium	10·6
Bulgaria	7·8
Czechoslovakia	3·7
Denmark	10·8
Finland	6·3
France	15·0
West Germany	13·7
Greece	12·3
Hungary	2·5
Ireland	18·5
Israel	10·4
Italy	24·4
Luxembourg	49·3
Malta	23·8
Monaco	140·8
Netherlands	10·3
Norway	23·0
Poland	21·2
Portugal	7·4
Romania	2·7
Spain	14·3

Sweden	12·0
Switzerland	41·0
Turkey	5·0
UK	13·8
Yugoslavia	7·6
Canada	14·6
USA	23·2
Japan	18·7
Ceylon	·2

It is clear from the table that smaller countries tend to have higher hotel beds per resident, other things being equal. Switzerland and Malta are particularly noticeable in this respect. However, because there is no international agreement as to what constitutes a hotel it is important not to misinterpret the table. The high figure for the US reflects the intensive use of hotels by residents rather than by overseas visitors.

If all these tables were refined, made more accurate and more comparable, it would be possible to see at a glance which countries had, for example, too few hotels for a given volume of traffic. It should also be possible to optimize the size of the tourist industry if it were possible to relate the diseconomies of excessive activity to particular ratios.

UK

This general picture of world tourism provides the background to tourism in the UK. Visits to the UK have risen slightly above the world average and the following table gives the figures since 1964,[11] and shows where the visitors come from.

Country of origin	Number of visits (thousands) to the UK			
	1964	1965	1966	1967
North America	767	897	1,048	1,104
Western Europe	1,342	1,472	1,643	1,822
Irish Republic	662	702	697	732
Other	486	526	579	631
Total	3,257	3,597	3,967	4,289
	1968	1969	1970	1971
North America	1,239	1,656	1,975	2,074
Western Europe	2,123	2,557	2,975	3,117
Irish Republic	783	764	743	721
Other	683	844	999	1,061
Total	4,828	5,821	6,692	6,973

Six countries – USA, Canada, West Germany, France, Netherlands and the Irish Republic – account for two thirds of our visitors. This pattern has remained virtually unchanged since the 1930s. In 1938 the ten most prolific suppliers of tourists – excluding the Commonwealth – supplied 81·02 per cent of total traffic. In 1967, they accounted for 79·98 per cent.[12] However, within this figure, the share of the United States has increased, and now one tourist in four is an American. This dependence on the USA for the bulk of UK tourist traffic is shared by other countries, in particular Ireland, Japan, Greece, W. Germany, Mexico and Canada. In all these countries, visitors from the USA exceed those from any other country.

The high percentage of the UK market accounted for by Americans is due to the size of the US population, rather than to the propensity of that population to visit the UK. Visits per 10,000 US residents to the UK are in fact lower than for residents of countries such as Sweden, Denmark, Switzerland, Belgium and the Netherlands.

In 1971, 1·6 million Americans visited the UK, a figure which has increased from 600,000 in 1964. Some way behind came France with 710,000, and then Germany with 698,000. The Commonwealth is still a great supplier of tourists; in 1971 some 179,000 came from Australia and New Zealand and 437,000 from Canada. The Irish Republic also supplied 721,000, but this statistic is not very reliable.

The importance of tourist expenditure in the UK is demonstrated by the fact that it currently generates more foreign currency than any visible export apart from machinery, transport equipment and chemicals. It is also the UK's largest earner of dollars.[13]

Export	1962	£m 1966	1970
Machinery			
(electrical and non-electrical)	1,111	1,429	1,946
Transport equipment	577	800	1,085
Chemicals	348	480	694
Textiles	250	271	361
Iron and steel	200	216	287
Metal manufactures	139	157	216
Tourism*	283	299	479

* includes fares paid to British Carriers

Tourism currently accounts for 11·6 per cent of invisible exports and 4·3 per cent of total exports. In spite of these large sums, the UK travel account was in the red up to 1967 owing to the even larger sums spent abroad by UK residents. In 1968, due partly to devaluation and to restrictions on spending overseas, a small surplus was recorded and the account has stayed in the black ever since.[14]

Year	Debits	Credits	Net
	£ million	£ million	£ million
1958	152	134	−18
1959	164	143	−21
1960	186	169	−17
1961	200	176	−24
1962	210	183	−27
1963	241	188	−53
1964	261	190	−71
1965	290	193	−97
1966	297	219	−78
1967	274	236	−38
1968	271	282	+11
1969	324	359	+35
1970	382	432	+50
1971	437	489	+52

Visitors to the UK have a high daily expenditure and stay longer than visitors to other European countries. This explains why the UK is able to extract from 5 million tourists almost as much foreign currency as Spain extracts from five times that number. The Americans are particularly high spenders, disposing of 55 per cent more per day than the average visitor.[15]

1971	All visitors	Visitors from USA
Average length of stay	14·7 days	11·0 days
Average expenditure per day	£4·7	£7·3
Average expenditure per visit	£69·1	£80·4

Further, the UK is more than holding its share of the tourist dollar which is spent in Europe. Americans are currently only spending ·6 per cent of total private consumption expenditure on international travel so the potential growth is enormous – bearing in mind that the average figure in OECD countries is higher at about 1·7 per cent.

The annual number of visits to the UK is probably not in itself too high; but too many visitors are in the same place at the same time. During 1969, London was visited by 64 per cent of all Dutch visitors to Britain, 73 per cent of Belgian visitors, 88 per cent of Swiss visitors and 85 per cent of French visitors.[16]

In London itself, a handful of attractions account for a high percentage of the visits – 93 per cent of all visitors going to Trafalgar Square, 85 per cent visiting Westminster Abbey, 83 per cent Buckingham Palace and 82 per cent the Tower of London.[17] The five most popular tourist attractions in the whole of the UK are in London, perhaps because over half of the visitors are coming to the UK for the first time. The tourist attractions outside London tend to be within a day's drive, thereby adding to the likelihood of the visitor spending his stay in a London hotel. 39 per cent of Americans visit Stratford, 37 per cent visit Oxford and 44 per cent visit Windsor.[18]

Geographical concentration is aggravated by seasonal concentration; over one third of overseas visits occur in July and August. 15 per cent of visits are made in August, yet only 3 per cent in February.[19] The UK is in fact better off than other European countries in this respect – particularly those which rely on the weather to attract visitors as this concentrates traffic even more in the hottest months. The situation could improve as second holidays – which are better distributed throughout the year – become more significant, and as physical limitations put a ceiling on the amount of traffic which can be accommodated in the peak months. The study of the seasonality of tourist traffic has received inadequate attention; it would however appear[20] that those countries which generate a small number of tourists – such as Spain – create a well-distributed flow; this is because the few that do travel come from the very top socio-economic groups, and their behaviour is not dictated by the incidence of paid holidays. Further, a large percentage is business traffic, which has a better seasonal distribution than non-business traffic. Looking at countries which generate more traffic, the seasonality of their traffic is more 'peaked'. This is because the growth has come from the lower socio-economic groups, who have less freedom of choice in the timing of their holidays, and because the percentage of traffic accounted for by business is smaller. There appears to be a third stage, which is reached when the economy of the tourist generating country has become post-industrial, and where average incomes are very high. Then seasonality becomes less 'peaked' due to relatively low percentages of the working population being occupied in manufacturing industries, where holidays tend to be fixed. Americans and the Swiss are entering this phase, and their visits are better spread throughout the year than the average.

The combined effect of geographical and seasonal concentration has influenced the location and profitability of the UK tourist industry – and in particular the hotels. Surveys by the English Tourist Board have shown London hotels to be the ones with the highest annual occupancy, and hotels in seaside resorts to be the least profitable. Of the 16 million nights spent by overseas visitors in UK hotels in 1967, 12 million were spent in hotels in London.[21] Yet nearly half of those visiting the UK for a holiday do not cross the threshold of a hotel. Of those that do, only a few spend more than 50 per cent of their stay in a hotel.

Americans are the most intensive hotel users – over 80 per cent of them spending some time in a hotel. Austrians are the least likely to stay in a hotel – a mere 7 per cent of their nights in the UK are spent in them.[22]

The business visitor is a more intensive user of hotels than the non-business visitor. Over a quarter of nights spent in hotels by overseas visitors are accounted for by business visitors, although they only account for 9 per cent of visits.[23]

This growth of overseas visits and activity, doubling approximately every seven years, has coincided with virtual stagnation of the domestic holiday market, up only 50 per cent in twenty years. The number of holidays taken by the British in GB is shown in the next table together with the numbers of holidays taken overseas.[24]

There would be no tourist problem if the flats, bed-sits and guest-houses on the coast, abandoned by the British holiday-

Numbers of Holidays (millions)

Year	Britain	Index	Abroad	Index	Total	Index
1951	25	100	1·5	100	26·5	100
1955	25	100	2	133	27	106
1960	31·5	126	3·5	234	35	132
1965	30	120	5	324	35	132
1970	34·5	138	5·75	384	40·3	152
1971	34	136	7·25	483	41·25	155
1972	37·5	150	8·5	567	46·0	174

maker, were now occupied by the overseas tourist. But they are not; and whereas the British holiday-makers spread the holidays – geographically – very well, the overseas visitor does not. So the stagnation of the domestic market and the fast growth of the overseas market has led to pressure on a small number of areas particularly popular with the overseas visitor – and this is the nub of the problem.

The domestic market is still the larger, though it is not growing so fast. In 1971 Britons took more than 130 million trips away from home (as opposed to holidays) and spent £1,800 million.[25] 120 million of these trips were in the UK and expenditure on these amounted to £1,220 million – as opposed to the £491 million spent in the UK by some 7 million overseas visitors. Business trips and trips to attend conferences accounted for 14 million of the 120 million trips, and £220 million of the £1,220 million expenditure. Of the 106 million non-business domestic visits, roughly half lasted between one and three nights and 75 per cent of these were visiting friends and relatives. The other half were holidays, the seasonality of which is a serious problem; 90 per cent of domestic holidays in the UK are taken in the months from June to September inclusive, and two thirds of main holidays are taken in July and August. In spite of constant and expensive campaigns by the British Tourist Authority over the last twenty years to get a better 'spread' this pattern has remained virtually unchanged. Within this peak, there is a more serious concentration in the last week in July and the first week in August. Nearly a quarter of holidays begin in that fortnight, and within that fortnight, nearly two thirds begin on a Saturday.

A national committee was set up by the Ministry of Labour and National Service in 1947 to deal with the problem, and in 1954 the

BTA organized a conference of all branches of educational activities to see if holiday and examination dates could be varied. In the words of the BTA itself, 'There was however no positive result arising from this conference.' In 1960, the government Social Survey commissioned a study[26] to throw light on the reasons for this concentration. This showed how misdirected previous efforts to spread the load had been. The BTA in particular had thought that price was an important determinant of holiday timing, and had exhorted the trade to reduce prices in the off-season. In reply to the question in the survey 'If you were completely free to choose, in what months of the year would you prefer to take your holiday' cheapness was the second least important consideration. Weather, and the length of the day, were the two most important reasons, and this explains why efforts to move the load have always failed.

To get the peak away from the beginning of August, the date of the August Bank Holiday was changed in 1967 from the beginning to the end of August. The BTA annual report for the following years plaintively records that 'the pressure during this period (22 July – 7 August) was greater in 1967 than in 1966'.

Another misconception concerned the importance of school holidays. Contrary to popular opinion, the Social Survey showed that educational considerations were less than half as important as employment factors – 57 per cent of main holiday starts were found to be determined by an employer's decision. The survey also concluded that people wanted to 'build up' for winter, and for this reason it will always be difficult to change habits.

Given the importance of the weather as a determinant, it is interesting to note that, on average, only four months of the year are wetter than July and August, and that May has more hours of sunshine than the popular holiday months.[27] The only respect in which the weather from June to September excels is in the daily mean temperature at sea-level – these four months are 20 per cent warmer than the other months in the summer.

There are however reasons for believing that the seasonality of domestic holidays, as of overseas holidays, will improve. The trend of employment away from manufacturing industry to the service sector will help. Manufacturing industries tend to close during summer, whereas the service industries spread holidays more evenly throughout the year. Secondly, the growth of second holidays, the most dynamic section of the market, will build up the incidence of holiday taking in the off-peak months, thereby securing a better seasonal distribution. The geographical concentration of domestic holidays, though much less acute than overseas visits, still gives cause for concern. The South-West, South and South-East of England account for nearly half of holiday destinations;[28] since 88 per cent of visits to the South-West are based on the sea, this means an intense concentration on the seaside resorts in Devon and Cornwall. Further, since 73 per cent of holiday-makers travel by car[29] – as against 47 per cent in 1960, the roads in that part of the country are highly congested in holiday time.

Hotels are no longer as popular as they were with holiday-makers; less formal types of accommodation – in particular camping and caravans – have benefited from the post-war growth in holidays away from home.[30] Even the holiday-camp may now be beginning to fall into disfavour.

Accommodation used on main holidays in Great Britain

	1965	1970
	%	%
Licensed hotel, motel	13	15
Unlicensed hotel etc.	28	16
Friends', relatives' home	25	24
Caravan	13	18
Rented accommodation	8	11
Holiday camp	6	6
Camping	4	6
Paying guest	3	7
	100	103*

(* The totals exceed 100 per cent because some holiday-makers use more than one category of accommodation.)

The future of the UK tourist industry does not rest with the domestic visitor but with the overseas visitor. Although in terms of expenditure the domestic visitor is still predominant, the next decade will increasingly see him take both his main and second holidays overseas, while the overseas visitor will come to the UK in ever-increasing numbers.

The real beneficiaries of the growth in UK demand have been the tourist industries overseas.[31]

Principal country visited	Number of visits (thousands)							
	1964	1965	1966	1967	1968	1969	1970	1971
United States	92	98	108	126	137	151	164	189
Canada	44	49	59	86	72	84	92	112
France	724	829	864	918	754	919	1,059	1,395
W. Germany	327	373	405	434	452	525	568	541
Italy	618	703	756	637	538	604	653	635
Belgium and Luxembourg	315	318	294	329	306	324	326	405
Netherlands	235	260	292	301	314	375	397	403
Austria	234	245	295	284	271	246	356	346
Denmark, Norway and Sweden	163	174	203	210	215	217	149	278
Switzerland	319	348	331	309	272	302	337	345
Spain	709	803	958	1,060	1,282	1,506	1,583	1,975
Other Western Europe	187	223	276	258	253	330	402	539
Other non-sterling area	105	143	165	165	194	214	235	264
Irish Republic*	1,608	1,649	1,596	1,692	1,766	1,743	1,532,	1,411
Australia and New Zealand	14	15	18	18	17	23	25	32
South Africa	15	16	16	21	21	27	29	33
Other sterling area	87	117	170	216	164	355	334	337
All countries**	5,897	6,472	6,918	7,202	7,269	8,083	8,482	9,426

* Statistics not very reliable.
** Includes holidays on cruise ships not assigned to any country.

Expenditure over the period has risen from £261 million in 1964 to £437 million in 1971. Of the 8·1 million visits in 1969 5·3 million were holiday visits, 1·2 million were business visits, the balance being miscellaneous visits. Of the 3·8 million holiday visits to Western Europe, half were on inclusive tours.

Tourism is increasingly an international phenomenon; the problems that it creates are due principally to the relentless growth rate, but are aggravated by seasonal and geographical concentration. As population increases, as incomes rise, as paid holidays lengthen, as the real cost of air travel falls, so growth will continue. Do we know how to control and direct it? Are we certain that we want it? The chapters that follow look for some answers.

5 The Structure of the Tourist Industry

The title of this chapter is misleading if it encourages the reader to believe that an industry with a recognizable shape and neatly inter-locking components has emerged in response to the demands analysed in previous chapters. Perhaps the major problem with tourism is that various sections of it have grown at speed, and other sections, which ought to have grown equally fast to prevent bottlenecks, have not done so. These differential growth rates have led to an overall structure with several weak links. For example, aircraft movements have grown faster than the ability of airports to handle them; travel to certain destinations has grown faster than their ability to absorb tourists; motorized tourism to various Eastern European countries has preceded by several years the investment in roads necessary to carry it; sales of caravans and camping equipment have grown faster than the facilities to absorb them. To oversimplify the problem, private expenditure on tourism has grown faster than the public investment to support it, and the structure has become decidedly top heavy.

These problems arise largely because tourists need a different infrastructure from residents. The homes, cars and offices vacated by the resident population when they go away on holiday are not filled by incoming tourists. If they were, then the tourist problem would simply be one of transporting people from one country to another and taking back an equivalent number as replacements. The fact that different infrastructures are needed for the resident and visitor is the very kernel of the matter. Further, it means that even if the world population remained stable, many of the problems of a rising population can be reproduced by greater mobility of a constant population. This can be demonstrated quite easily; imagine a society of ten families each living in one flat in a block of ten flats. Initially, none of them can afford a holiday away from home so there are no hotels, and the occupancy of the accommodation stock – the ten flats – is 100 per cent. As this modest society prospers, two families can afford to take a holiday away from home – unfortunately at the same time – and two hotel suites are built for their fortnight's holiday. The occupancy rate of the accommodation stock then falls to 83 per cent, as ten families need twelve units of accommodation. When two more families move into the income bracket which can support a fortnight's holiday, there is no problem as they can fortunately use the existing hotel suites. But when the fifth and sixth families wish to take a holiday in the only sunny month, one more hotel suite has to be constructed and the occupancy rate of the accommodation stock falls to 77 per cent as ten families need thirteen units.

This oversimplified illustration of the effect of mobility on accommodation requirements shows how a more affluent society needs a different infrastructure from a less affluent one – and also needs more of it. More hotels mean more electricity cables, water mains, telephone wires, television aerials, and more of the general clutter which accompanies development.

Few countries have managed to achieve a balanced infrastructure for their own residents – particularly as far as housing is concerned; small wonder that the infrastructure for visitors is seldom balanced and that the public sector is usually responsible.

Having identified these structural problems, it is quite a different matter to solve them. Public ownership of all the components of the tourist industry is clearly inappropriate as, by and large, it is the public sector that has proved inadequate. Less formalized coordination within the framework of an indicative plan is difficult owing to the international nature of tourism. How can UK planners guess how many overseas visitors will want to camp in the UK in ten years' time?

Three partial solutions are detectable; firstly, there is considerable vertical integration within the industry which in itself tends to strengthen the weak links. Airlines are investing in hotels; tour operators are buying travel agents. This will be examined in detail later in this chapter. Secondly, more countries are drawing up tourist plans, from which the various component parts of the tourist industry can derive likely demand for their own goods and services. This again tends to lead to coherent development of the industry. (If the plan is wrong, then of course everyone is in trouble.) Thirdly, the public sector is bestirring itself and beginning to make good defects in infrastructure.

The second and third solutions are dealt with in later chapters; this chapter looks at the first and examines the main components of the tourist industry; this is done in the approximate order in which the tourist comes into contact with them but it is by no means a comprehensive list. It looks at the travel agent, the tour operator, the airport, the airline, the accommodation industry, and finally miscellaneous services at the destination, such as carhire, and tourist attractions. The vertical integration which is taking place is particularly highlighted because of its possible contribution to the solution of the structural problems outlined earlier.

The Travel Agent

It is one of the more unkind paradoxes of the travel industry that the body of gentlemen who, following in the footsteps of Thomas Cook, have done so much to instil the travel habit in the public's mind should now be those whose very existence is most threatened by the expansion and development of their industry. Of the various components of the travel industry, the 1,500 U K travel agencies with their 2,500 retail outlets are now the most vulnerable and most dispensable. In the 'good old days', when travel abroad was complicated and the various components of a trip had to be laboriously assembled to suit the requirements of the well-heeled individual customer, the services of a travel agent were essential. Carriers and customers alike relied on him. Nowadays both are beginning to desert him; the carriers tend to regard him as an expensive, inefficient and unnecessary middleman between themselves and their customers; and the customer often finds it quicker, more convenient and sometimes cheaper to deal direct with the carrier. The agent is being squeezed from both sides, and the reasons for this are worth examining.

Firstly, advance booking is becoming less necessary for many kinds of travel. Air travel is becoming more like rail travel and bus travel, with the customer making his arrangements at short notice and often able to get on the next plane. If he is unwilling to take the risk of going straight to the airport, he can telephone the airline direct and reserve a seat. Because of IATA (International Air Transport Association) arrangements, the airline can book him on a competitor's flight if unable to accommodate him itself. The answer is available to him more quickly than if he went through an agent. Further, credit facilities are often easier as the airline accepts credit cards when the travel agent does not.

Although airlines still depend on the agent for some 77 per cent of sales of airline tickets, they are discretely encouraging this trend to 'spontaneous' travel through their fare structure, charging reduced rates for standby flights. Laker Airways is attempting to extend 'walk-on' flights for transatlantic travel and it is only a matter of time before they or someone else succeeds. This trend to less formality – inevitable as air travel becomes more commonplace – means that the agent is increasingly by-passed. Indeed the older travel agent has seen it all happen before with rail travel, from which he used to derive nearly all his commission and which is now of negligible importance.

Secondly, the tour operators are beginning to suspect that the travel agent is an unnecessary overhead in the sale of their package holidays. It is the operator who bears the advertising costs, and who takes the risk if all the package holidays are not sold. With margins under constant competitive pressure, and profits often less than 1 per cent of turnover, a 10 per cent saving on agent's commission is too good an opportunity to miss. Since agent's commission totalled £12 million on inclusive tours in 1970 and the operators lost £1·6 million, it is only natural that the latter should seek to redress the balance.

Although they may not admit to it publicly, many tour operators are now encouraging the public to deal direct and some of the smaller ones do not use agents at all. Whereas the tour operator used to be dependent on the travel agent, the situation is now being reversed. Indeed, tour operators are being more selective as they cut down the number of travel agents they deal with.

Thirdly, the travel agent is losing the confidence of the public as well as its custom. When BEA announced proposals to halve airfares on many European routes in September 1971, travel

agents denounced the scheme as 'diabolical' and 'appalling'
Popular opinion on the other hand welcomed the suggestions
being in the consumers' interest. Similarly, when Laker Airway
'Skytrain' – offering transatlantic travel at £35 with no booking
was approved by the Civil Aviation Authority, the Association c
British Travel Agents issued a statement that 'it was not in th
public's interest'.[2] Because the travel agent is paid commission, h
is naturally against reduction in tariffs; he is reluctant to explai
to the customer about advance purchasing systems, group di:
counts etc., which may cost him half his commission. For th
reason other sections of the travel industry – such as affinit
groups – who promote cheaper travel will increasingly benefit z
the expense of the travel agent.

The *Sunday Times* showed how many travel agents – includin
many belonging to the official trade association, The Associatio
of British Travel Agents – were overcharging customers o
scheduled flights.[3] Many customers also resent the high level c
commission paid to travel agents on related purchases; one schem
offering insurance pays the travel agent 35 per cent commission.

Fourthly, as the general public becomes better educated, mor
travelled and more familiar with the countries it visits, so it is les
dependent on the advice and reassurance of the travel agent.

Fifthly, other outlets have started to sell the travel agent's mai
revenue earner, the package tour. They are often able to do thi
more effectively and conveniently than the travel agent. In thi
respect, perhaps the banks pose the major threat. They have
captive high-street clientele, good locations, access to credit, an
are heavily computerized – an essential if a quick and efficien
service to the travelling public is to be offered in the future. In th
USA, Australia and Holland they have invaded the travel industr
in style. In Holland in 1970, there were 600 travel agents. Ther
are now 6,000 as the banks have joined, and they have creame
the market by handling the highly profitable package tours.

The signs of this invasion are now visible in the UK. Nationa
and Grindlays Bank are already members of ABTA (Associatio
of British Travel Agents) through their ownership of Cox & Kings
Britain's oldest travel firm. The Bank of New South Wales ha
applied for membership and others will doubtless follow. Barclay

Bank already sells travel insurance over the counter, and the largest shareholder in Thomas Cook's is the Midland Bank, which will be selling travel through its 2,600 outlets.

On the continent, other retailers have began to sell package holidays. Gelmoli, one of the largest Swiss department stores, sells package holidays at forty-one branches and is contemplating including them in its mail order catalogue. In France, Shell sell a wide range of travel facilities at 100 petrol stations; and twenty of them are linked to the Citel International Hotel Reservation Network, a facility few travel agents can offer.

Competition from these sources is bound to increase and it is difficult to see how – or indeed why – it should be resisted in the UK. Tesco's, Woolworth's and Marks & Spencer's may all be selling inclusive tours by the end of the decade. W. H. Smith's are already doing so.

Finally, the changing structure of the industry is squeezing out the independent travel agent. Tour operators and airlines are taking over travel agencies to integrate vertically, and those that do not acquire travel agencies are increasingly able to offer the traveller accommodation, car-hire and other facilities themselves. An airline can often assemble a package for the independent traveller as quickly and efficiently as the agent. Use of the computer for all forms of reservations will also squeeze out the independent agent who is unable to afford a computer terminal. More important, the development and distribution by world airlines of automated credit cards which will activate vending machines in airports and enable passengers to issue themselves with tickets, confirmed and ready to use, is a further step towards eliminating the travel agent from the scene.

The traditional travel agents are therefore under severe pressure; although they operate in a market which is expanding fast, many of them are making less money than they used to do. The usual reaction of the trade to this predicament is summed up by the President of The French Association of Travel Agents, M. Maurice Brillant[5] 'A new legal structure for the travel industry . . . is needed because the retail travel agent is being forced into a weaker position through increased competition from banks, supermarkets and petrol stations.' He went on to argue that 'as a syndi-

cate we must continue to fight for higher commission.' But th
reason the travel agent is being forced into a weaker position i
by and large, because his function can either be dispensed with, o
performed more efficiently by someone else. The demand for highe
and higher commission, far from the solution to the travel agent'
problem, would actually hasten his demise.

Tour Operators

Half the total foreign travel movements from the UK are nov
accounted for by package tours (of the five million holiday visit
to Western Europe in 1971, three million were on inclusive tours
and in 1971 the industry's turnover was £170 million. If the trave
agent is the retailer, selling tourist goods and services to the cus
tomer, then the tour operator is the wholesaler. He supplies to th
retailer packages which he in turn has acquired from the manu
facturers – the airlines and the hotels – and put together. As witl
many wholesalers in the distributive trades, the tour operato
would dearly like to deal direct with the public – through ma
order or even on stands in a supermarket, and save the retailer'
margin of 10 per cent; but as yet they are not ready to say s
publicly in view of their current dependence on the travel agent fo
custom. 85 per cent of inclusive tours (packaged holidays) in th
UK are still sold through independent retailers.

The economics of the tour operating business are such that th
larger units have a distinct advantage over the smaller ones an
they are consequently increasing their share of the market
Between 1970 and 1971, the percentage of total inclusive tou
seats applied for by the three largest companies increased fron
33·5 per cent to 42·4 per cent. By 1972 these three tour operators
Clarksons (the largest tour operator in the world), Thomsons an
Horizon – accounted for over 50 per cent of the inclusive tours sol
in the UK. The other 67 tour operators share the remaining 5
per cent.

There are several reasons why this section of the industry i
dominated by larger units. Firstly, they are in a stronger bargain
ing position *vis-à-vis* the airlines and hotels, and can secure bette
terms for buying in bulk and for paying in advance. The large

our operators have beaten some Spanish hoteliers down to 40p per day for full board for their holiday-makers. These competitive prices enable them to undercut the smaller firms, and thus increase their share of a market which is sensitive to price changes.

Secondly, the larger units can indulge in expensive advertising campaigns which are beyond the means of their smaller rivals. In 1972, Clarksons spent £1 million on press and T V advertising and on producing 12 million copies of all their literature. In order to sell 500,000 holidays, Thomsons spend £600,000 on 3 million brochures, £200,000 on television advertising, £200,000 on press advertising, and £40,000 on cinema advertising – over £1 million before a single holiday was sold. Horizon print 3 million brochures to sell 300–400,000 holidays, and Global 1·8 million to sell 190,000. Overall in 1971 some 23 million brochures were produced at a cost of about £3 million to sell 3 million holidays. At £1 per head per customer carried, this is a substantial overhead and an entry fee which few companies can afford.

Thirdly, the larger companies have access to substantial resources; this can finance vertical integration, i.e. the acquisition of hotels and airlines, which in turn enables them to streamline their operations and cut their costs. This finance also enables them to survive lean patches. These resources are usually available from parent companies. Thus Thomson Holidays can look to the Thomson Organization, which derives a mere 7 per cent of its profits from travel; Clarksons have Shipping Industrial Holdings to lean on; Leroy-Whitehall is owned by British and Commonwealth Shipping, and Blue Sky by British Caledonian Shipping. Even Thomas Cook now has the Midland Bank's resources behind it.

Since the industry is not always a profitable one, the existence of giant holding companies in the background is of crucial importance. Information disclosed by the Air Transport Licensing Board and the Civil Aviation Authority showed that the fifty-six tour operators concerned lost a net £1·62 million in 1970 and a net £8·72 million in 1971. In the latter year, nineteen companies contrived to lose £9·6 million and the remaining thirty-seven only made £0·9 million profit. On a total turnover of £170 million this is a poor performance, for which the larger companies are chiefly responsible.[6]

The chief problem is the high occupancy rates which tou operators have to achieve in order to break even. For many, 9 per cent occupancy is break even point; comparable percentage for scheduled airlines, hotels and railways are approximately 6 per cent, 50 per cent and 40 per cent respectively. While size may bring with it some advantages, it clearly means that mistakes ar very expensive.

As the larger companies increase their share of a growing mar ket, it is likely that computer-based systems will replace th creaking manual systems currently in use. It has been estimate that these manual systems can cope with 75,000 bookings annuall but no more. Several tour operators now sell more than this, an Leasco, a computer manufacturing company, has invested £ million on their behalf in Trunks (Tour Reservations Unite Kingdom Systems Ltd). This system is expensive; even with th largest company it would cost £1·15 per booking, but if problems o sharing can be overcome, this cost could be reduced. This system will give the potential customer an instant response on availabilit and will offer alternative holidays if the first choice is fully booked It will also give management better control over their operation by identifying slow-moving holidays. The location of compute terminals for this system will be an important issue as travel agent unable to afford one will be at a disadvantage compared wit those that can.

Tour operators are diversifying into other markets; for exampl the conference market, where margins are wider and the seasona spread more even. Conferences can now be held in Majorca at £2 per head.

In spite of its reputation as an industry of profitless growth outside interests appear keen to have a stake in it. As with th travel agency business, banks are buying their way in. America Express, the US banking and travel group, own 19 per cent o Clarksons, and have options to own 49 per cent. This is a goo illustration of the way control of the tourist industry is being bought by international or multinational companies. Retailers ar similarly diversifying to package holidays. Great Universal Store own Global, and Migros – the Swiss store – owns Hotelplan another tour operator.

In the same way as the large tour operators have their own airlines, so some of the larger airlines are buying tour operators. For example, in 1970 BOAC purchased 56 per cent of the equity of Alta Travel Ltd to develop special interest tours, professionally escorted holidays and expeditions.

In spite of the problems facing the tour operating industry – chiefly how to convert the growth in customers into growth of profits through correct pricing – the future should be rosy. At the moment, a relatively small number of UK adults take holidays overseas – some 3 million in 1970 – and while the volume has been increasing steadily in recent years, saturation point is still a long way off. The percentage could rise from about $12\frac{1}{2}$ per cent of all adults taking holidays overseas now to 40 per cent in 1980, which would involve transporting some 15 million adults overseas. An increasing proportion of these will travel on inclusive tours and the majority of them will be carried by two or possibly three operators in aircraft which they own and staying in hotels which they have helped to finance. The more distant holiday destinations, such as the West Indies and the Far East, will increasingly be included in the tour operator's catalogue and travel to such places is likely to increase at a faster rate than to European ones. Another major growth area for the tour operator is in winter holidays. The number of packaged winter holidays has grown from 6,900 in 1963–4 (October to March) to, according to *The Times* of 9 November 1972, about 1·2 million in 1972–3. Now that price controls for winter holidays are being dismantled, further growth is inevitable. The increase in summer holidays has led to an increase in the amount of holiday plant which is idle in the winter months, and the relaxation of price control means that these can be sold at marginal prices in winter. By definition, there must be more first holidays than second holidays, and as the situation is reached where everyone who wants a holiday takes one, further growth can only come from second holidays.

A small cloud on the tour operators' horizon is government intervention to safeguard the interests of the public. The Civil Aviation Act includes powers to introduce a system of licensing of holiday tour operators – a system which many other countries already have. The Trade Association, ABTA, professes to be ready to discipline and expel any tour operator who is guilty of bad behaviour, but in spite of substantiated complaints on many occasions, no member has suffered more than a friendly admonishment. If their house is not put in order by the tour operators themselves this task will be done for them.

Airports

There is of course a price to be paid for the breakthrough in packaged holidays by air; cheap, fast and quiet air travel has meant expensive, slow and noisy airports. If ever there was a need for a coherent and consistent policy covering the whole of the tourist industry so that its component parts could grow at mutually compatible rates and so that planning for the industry as a whole could be integrated with other national plans, that need is proved by the history of post-war airport development in the UK. For a country of its size, the UK has more airports than any other Western European country; yet their distribution and development have taken place with no reference to any national airport plan; with little reference to growth in aircraft movements and changing aviation technology; in isolation – or defiance of regional development plans; in blind disregard of the peace and comfort of those who live in their vicinity; and often in apparent ignorance of the presence of other airports in the same catchment areas.

Twenty-five years ago, it seemed that these mistakes were going to be avoided; in 1945 a White Paper was issued with the intention of ensuring the 'orderly expansion of air transport'.[7] It stated that airfields required for scheduled air services – at that time often owned and run by local authorities – should be acquired and managed by the Ministry of Civil Aviation. The post-war Labour Government took the view that State control was essential to ensure the orderly development of airports in relation to traffic growth and changes in aircraft technology, and that the State alone could provide adequate resources for this balanced development. In 1947, the government therefore announced that it was going to acquire forty-six airports.

During the 1950s, however, this policy was unfortunately abandoned, and then reversed. In the 1955/6 Parliamentary Session, the Select Committee on Estimates – not perhaps the best qualified body to pronounce on this subject – examined the question of civil airports, and recommended that municipalities be encouraged to acquire and operate their own airports. This policy of decentralization was eventually adopted and set out in a White Paper in 1961.[8] Thereafter, the government took positive steps to sell airports to local authorities, in the belief that this would encourage a more commercial approach to airport operation. This has inevitably meant that, over the past twenty years, a coherent national policy for airports has been neither formulated nor implemented. *Ad hoc* development of individual airports has taken place with no conception of their role in the overall pattern of national and international transport. So much was in fact admitted on 26 January 1971 in evidence to the Select Committee on Nationalized Industries when it examined the affairs of the British Airports Authority – set up in 1966 to manage the three London airports and Prestwick. The Under-Secretary at the Department of Trade and Industry responsible for this side of civil aviation policy said 'We cannot have local ownership, local responsibility and a highly centralized direction on what is to happen to airports.'

The result of this policy – or absence of policy – is that there are now some areas of the UK which merit an airport but which do not have one; and others which merit an airport and which have two or – in some cases – three. If a national airport policy had existed, there would not now be airports at both Prestwick and Abbotsinch; Birmingham and Coventry; Liverpool and Manchester; Southampton and Bournemouth; Newcastle and Teesside; Cardiff and Bristol. The Edwards Committee[9] put their finger on the problem. 'There is little doubt too that in more than one case civic pride has galloped ahead of cold economic assessment with some waste of resources.'[10] Since Liverpool Corporation took over the operation of Liverpool Airport in 1961 it has lost £3 million and the annual deficit is £700,000. Closing the airport would bring little relief to the ratepayers of Liverpool; they would still have to find £430,000 annually for thirty years to service the debt. The Corporation has tried to sell the airport but, understandably, it has limited attractions as an investment. The

Corporation is therefore investing a further £10 million, which will increase the annual loss to £1·5 million.

A national airport policy would have avoided this waste of resources. It would also have avoided the confusion of the past few years which has clouded the future of areas such as Gatwick, Cublington, Luton, Stansted and Foulness. Again, the Edwards Committee points its finger at the culprit:

> To forecast our national airport needs, and then to create and develop the facilities, is bound to be a very difficult exercise. But although it is easy to exaggerate what could, in fact, be achieved by a study in depth, it is worse to tackle each problem on a purely *ad hoc* basis. One can at least show whether decisions and projected decisions are consistent with one another.[11]

Two years later, the Select Committee referred to above were more direct about the problem. 'Your Committee regret the present dilatoriness in starting to prepare a National Plan.'[12]

The Edwards Report bears a distressing resemblance to sections of the Rochdale Report[13] on the ports some ten years earlier – distressing both because the lesson of the ports has clearly not been learnt and distressing because of its confirmation of this country's inability to coordinate its transport plans. The Rochdale Committee had this to say:

> We have become increasingly aware in the course of our inquiry that a fundamental defect in the organisation of ports in this country is the lack of any central planning. . . We think that there is an urgent need for some central machinery to co-ordinate and supervise the execution of plans for the development of the harbours of Great Britain on a national basis.[14]

The Edwards Committee described in similar terms what a National Airports Plan should achieve, and it is worth setting out their ideas as they identify the problems to date and act as a reminder that over five years after they reported, no work on the plan has yet commenced.

The objectives for a National Airports Plan might be summarised as follows: (i) to achieve a distribution of airports which will meet the needs of economically viable or socially supported air services in every part of the country, without wasting scarce resources in view of the large amounts of capital and areas of land required for development; (ii) to prevent a proliferation of airports serving the same traffic areas, and thus to strengthen the economics of the airports themselves and to provide the basis for a stronger network of air services than would be possible if airlines served two or more airports where one could suffice; (iii) to ensure greater co-ordination between airport development and the provision of air services, so that investment decisions in neither field are made without knowledge of decisions in the other; (iv) to establish forward plans for meeting future requirements – particularly those arising from the rapidly changing operational characteristics of civil aircraft; (v) to co-ordinate airport development with the development of means of access to airports.[15]

One final paragraph drove the point home:

We recommend that those who have the duty to issue licences and to fashion a coherent airline industry should also have the task of long-term research into, and planning of, airport policy. If this country is to avoid some of the problems arising on the eastern seaboard of the US, continuous and professional study of airport development is essential.[16]

While the Edwards Committee had a clear idea of the importance of a national airport policy and plan, they did not pursue the logic of their own arguments to the next stage – that of arguing that a national airport plan itself must be consistent with other national objectives. Instead, they took as their starting point that 'the primary long-term objective of government policy towards civil aviation should be to ensure that the customer, be it for personal travel or freight, should be able to buy what he wants at the minimum economic price compatible with safety.'[17] Such a policy of continuing to meet demand for air travel in the cheapest possible way can only lead to environmental disaster; so much has in fact already been admitted by opting for Maplin instead of Cublington as the site of London's third airport, and paying a substantial economic penalty of the order of £150 million in passenger-user costs to avoid serious blight on the environment of central southern England. This interaction of transport and tourism with other national objectives should be explicitly acknowledged when airport policy is reviewed by the new Civil Aviation Authority.

As a result of past policies, there are now about 100 licensed civil airports in the UK used by forty million people in 1971, but only forty-six of these airports have facilities which can be used by scheduled air transport services. In 1969, these forty-six handled 32 million passengers – double the number for 1961. Traffic is highly concentrated within these forty-six airports, twelve of them accounting for nearly 90 per cent of passengers and 60 per cent of flights. The three London airports account for 61 per cent of passengers – a percentage which has been steadily increasing. There are now some 850 flights per day in the London area. Of the 32 million passengers, 19 million were on international services and 14 million of these passed through Heathrow and Gatwick – double the number of international passengers handled in New York and making London, by a substantial margin, the busiest centre of international air travel in the world. Put in a broader international context, the forty-two principal airports in Western Europe handled 114 million passengers in 1969. Twelve airports accounted for over 50 per cent of these and one, Heathrow, accounted for 17 per cent of the total.

As is suggested in other parts of this book, the tourist is often the unwitting and undeserving recipient of many subsidies from central government. One such subsidy comes to him via airport authorities for, according to the Chairman of the British Airports Authority, his is the only airport authority in the world which makes a profit. Overall, UK airports apart from Heathrow lost £2·6 million in the year ending March 1968.

The 1971 Heathrow profit of £8·2 million is itself a statistic of doubtful legality. It excludes, for a start, the annual loss which the airport costs those who live near it. 'One way is to assess the disamenity to local inhabitants in terms of house value loss and cost of moving; for London Airport (Heathrow) this comes to about £60 million per year'.[18] Secondly, the profit was only arrived at after receiving £9·8 million in rents and trading concessions. Large sums can only be demanded by the airport authorities if the concessionaires at the airports pre-empt for themselves the duty-free concessions intended for their customers. A bottle of Scotch whisky normally bears duty at £2·20 and can be purchased for £2·50. The thirsty traveller, expecting to purchase a duty-free bottle for 30p, is in for a rude shock. At Heathrow it costs £1·25 and the traveller's only consolation is that the duty-free whisky on the Bergen line car-ferry is £2.[19] Thirdly, any surplus on airport management is comfortably outweighed by the cost of air navigational services. In 1968 this cost was £12·2 million, against a total surplus on airports of £1·5 million. Again, this is another unwitting subsidy to the tourist.

Outside the UK, the traveller is subsidized by the taxpayers of the country he visits. In the USA, the Federal Government has authority to meet up to 50 per cent of capital investment for airport developments which are included in the National Airport Plan. The Civil Aeronautics Board endeavours to justify government assistance to airports by saying 'it should properly be regarded as primarily a subsidy for the benefit of the public and the cities served rather than for the benefit of the airlines.' Whatever the intention, the practical effect is either to boost airline profits or to save the travelling public money, both at the expense of the non-travelling public.

In Europe, there are a wide variety of methods of assisting those who run the airports and, through them, the airlines and their passengers. In some cases, the capital is provided free and in others no allowance is required for depreciation. Often, a straightforward loss is accepted by the government and made good. In the words of the Edwards Committee, 'In summary, it seems that, on a full accounting basis, the majority of European airports are not making an economic return on investment.'[20]

It is therefore clear that those who live in the area of airports and the taxpayer at large are subsidizing the traveller by a substantial sum. While the airlines have been able to bring down the cost of air travel to their passengers by using larger and faster aircraft and have passed on the savings to the traveller, these very developments have increased costs at the terminals. However, because of the fragmented nature of the industry, passengers have had the benefit of reduced travel costs, but have been shielded from the higher terminal costs through airport subsidies. The construction of a new airport at Maplin is likely to continue this form of subsidy. The social or economic justification for this is very difficult to perceive; indeed, the British Airports Authority has the highest profits target of any nationalized industry in the UK precisely because it has no social obligations whatsoever. The airport and runways at Maplin are likely to cost £600 million and, with the British Airports Authority currently clearing profits of £3·9 million per annum,[21] it will clearly need substantial assistance. The prospects of the taxpayer getting a return on this investment are as rosy as his hope of making money on Concorde. The *Financial Times* put its finger on the reason why this massive investment was necessary. 'Without a tourist industry which will almost certainly be attracting 10 million tourists to Britain within four years, there could be little or no need for an airport at Foulness.'[22] If this is the case, it is not unreasonable to ask the tourist industry to pay for the airport. Again, the Edwards Report points at the solution.

We believe that airports should aim to cover their full costs, including a commercial return on the capital investment, reflecting the level of risk involved in this particular type of enterprise. . . Our own view is that air services should in the long-term meet the full costs of all the facilities on which they depend.[23]

The decision to build at Maplin provides a good example of another of the themes of this chapter – the alarming tendency to deal with one section of the tourist industry with no regard to the consequences of a decision on other sections. The Roskill Commission justified the need for a third London airport by forecasting future demand for travel to the UK and relating that demand to existing capacity at London's airports. The forecast is far in excess of London's capacity to accommodate visitors and there is no point in them arriving at Maplin if there is nowhere for them to stay.

This same mistake has been committed more dramatically and less excusably in Antigua; it has a modern airport at Coolidge which, unlike the airports at the neighbouring islands, can accommodate large jet aircraft. Its competitive advantage therefore lies in mass tourism. However, it only boasts four hotels with more than fifty rooms, where the tariffs are £18 per night with air conditioning extra.

The future will bring with it many problems as far as airports are concerned. It is likely that public opinion will bring pressure to

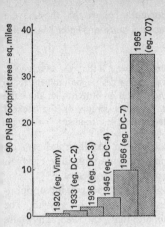

a. Growth of aircraft noise

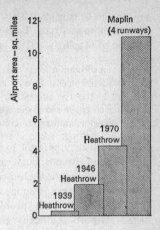

b. Growth of airport size

Figure 2.
Aircraft noise and airport size

bear on the traveller and make him pay the full costs of his travel. This trend is discernible through government attitudes to aircraft noise. Historically, the costs of noise have been borne by the community at large, who have simply had to put up with it. The scale of the problem of airport noise has been graphically described by J. E. Ffowcs Williams, Rolls Royce Professor of Theoretical Acoustics at Imperial College London. 'The human ear is attuned to the human voice; the sound energy of a large aircraft is one million times louder. All the world's population shouting in unison would generate the same sound level as a 707 at take-off.' The scale of the increase in aircraft noise is shown on Figure 2a.

In future, the travelling public will have to bear these noise costs, either by having to travel further to get to the newer and more remote airports or through the discomfort of steeper angles of descent, or by paying higher airfares to pay for quieter engines. The logic of this approach will ultimately lead to the removal of hidden subsidies at airports, with the costs gradually being shifted back to the traveller, where they rightly belong.

If this solution is to be adopted, the British Airports Authority will have to be educated. They currently believe that they have a divine right to a subsidy. Their recent Chairman, Peter Masefield, has said of Maplin.

> Even at a substantial early use of the runway, if that can be achieved, the airports income at today's level of charges seems unlikely to be sufficient to pay the interest on the capital employed – let alone the operating costs. Nor can the costs be borne simply on the back of the air transport industry in its international environment.

Why not? It may be right to subsidize a declining industry on humanitarian grounds; but it cannot be right to subsidize a growth industry which creates such environmental problems.

After the problem of public opinion and the growing unpopularity of airports is the problem of catering for growth. The British Airports Authority estimate that, by 1985, anywhere between 80 million and 130 million passengers per year could be using London's five existing airports. The figure for 1970 was 20 million. Aircraft movements are not forecast to rise so fast, due to the introduction of larger aircraft and to the higher densities achieved by chartered flights. Nonetheless, the BAA forecast a doubling of movements in the London area from 350,000 in 1970 to 6–800,000 in 1985.

The principal component of growth is likely to be charter traffic. Between June 1970 and June 1971, UK charter flights increased by 17 per cent and scheduled flights by only 2 per cent. Passengers increased by 31 per cent and 6 per cent respectively.[24] In 1970, there were about 4½ million charter passengers on flights to and from Europe. This should grow to 25 million by 1980. On the North American route, the figure should grow from 750,000 in 1970 to 6 million in the early 1980s.

Traffic growth on scheduled services presents enough problems; these are aggravated, as far as the airports are concerned, when charter traffic accounts for the growth. Such flights are more concentrated than scheduled flights into certain times of the year, certain times of the week, and even certain times of the day. The capital investment to meet peak demand is therefore substantially higher for a given number of passengers. One might also add that passengers on chartered flights are less likely to spend freely in the airport shops than passengers on the more expensive scheduled flights.

Historically, traffic growth has been accommodated by enlarging the capacity of existing airports; Figure 2b shows how Heathrow has grown over the last thirty years. This solution is no longer possible; in addition to the reasons already given there is a limit to the number of aircraft that can be handled with safety in the air above an airport, and land availability around existing airports is restricted. Future traffic growth, all over the world, is having to be handled at new airports, considerably larger than existing ones, at locations remote from the communities they serve.

This may bring with it the opportunity to close smaller airports near the cities and thus release valuable land for other purposes. It may also lead to some smaller countries closing their own international airports and providing instead a feeder service to another one. In the Caribbean, for example, each island is currently insisting on its own international airport, but economic logic may push them towards a more sensible alternative. These new airports are of course more than just airports; as with the proposed complex at Maplin, many will include a new town, a major industrial area and, where appropriate, a new port. In view of their accessibility, many could be new shopping centres catering for nearby urban areas and perhaps specializing in imported goods. Maplin will probably be the biggest single planning and development project ever undertaken in the UK, costing as much as £1,000 million and taking as long as twenty years to complete.

Other countries are faced with similar problems. In 1969 the Secretary of Transportation in the US Administration announced to an astonished audience that America needed 900 more airports in the next ten years – roughly a new airport every four days. Istanbul's Yesilkoy Airport currently handles $\frac{1}{4}$ million passengers per year, but it is being expanded to handle no less than 20 million. Developments on this scale can only lead to conflict with other objectives and highlight the necessity of putting the requirements of airports in some sort of framework instead of unquestioningly finding the land to meet the limitless desire of mankind to travel.

Airlines

In 1972, passengers on world scheduled airlines – excluding those of China and USSR – numbered 450 million.[25] Of these 450 million, 90 million were on international flights, an increase of 14 per cent on 1970. The operating expenses of those airlines totalled $23,000 million, $1,000 million of which was on in-flight catering. Between 1970 and 1974 they are likely to spend $30,000 million on new aircraft. The airline industry is therefore a sizeable economic force, even when the operations of the non-scheduled or charter airlines are left out. The largest airline in the world, in terms of passengers carried, is the Russian airline Aeroflot, which carried 75 million passengers in 1970. BEA is the seventh largest, carrying 8 million in 1970. The five airlines in between are all American.

Throughout the 1960s, the number of passengers carried by the scheduled airlines – which belong to the International Air Transport Association – increased by about 12 per cent annually. Recently, however, this increase has been less; between 1970 and 1971 it was only 2 per cent. The reason for this is not a fall in total passenger movements by air, but the syphoning off by the charter airlines, who are not members of IATA, of most of the growth. They have been able to do this by reducing fares, whereas the IATA members have agreed to keep fares at a higher level. The regulations concerning international airfares are complicated; in the words of the Edwards Committee, 'The structure of world civil aviation has been fashioned by many forces amongst which economic logic has played only a modest part.'[26]

Briefly, for reasons which may be valid but which have never been clearly demonstrated to be so, the scheduled airlines have agreed not to compete with each other. The price of travel, the width of the seats, the quantity of food supplied on the flight and even the charge for in-flight entertainment, are all agreed by the member airlines of IATA and ratified by their governments thereafter. Competition is therefore restricted and, to quote Bernard Levin, 'All airline advertising, like all petrol advertising, is based on an attempt to prove that two identical substances are in fact different.'[27] The constitution of IATA which was set up in 1945 is such that all decisions have to be unanimous; since the smaller airlines who need higher fares to remain viable can veto lower fares, the effect of IATA has been to keep fares at an artificially high level. The consumer has, however, benefited by being able to transfer from one flight to another without penalty, and by knowing that, come rain or shine, services will be maintained on a regular basis to the destinations served by IATA airlines. IATA also performs a task of enormous complexity in revising every two years 200,000 international airfares in eighty currencies for 107 airlines.

Yet the case against IATA is perhaps stronger. It has led to excess capacity on scheduled flights and hence to reduced profitability for the scheduled airlines (in 1971 the average passenger load factor on all scheduled flights was 50·8 per cent); it has brought about fare levels which are unrealistically high compared with those on charter flights and this has diverted traffic away from the scheduled airlines; it has deprived the customer of the beneficial results of competition and has led to complicated and unenforceable regulations – which have likewise discredited the industry in the eyes of the travelling public. It is very doubtful whether the existing structure can survive much longer.

The scheduled airlines tend to be government owned. Of the 107 IATA airlines, 42 are wholly government owned, 28 have some degree of government ownership and only 37 are privately owned. However, 15 of these are US airlines where the government keeps a paternal eye on them. By and large, losses on scheduled airlines represent subsidies from taxpayers to travellers, and these sums can be large; in 1971 the net loss of the world's scheduled airlines was 2·1 per cent of their revenues – a loss of nearly £200 million.[28] The pace in civil aviation over the past decade has therefore been set by the charter airlines, which do not belong to IATA. The start of the charter boom can in fact be traced back to the end of the Second World War, when ex-RAF pilots, complete with goggles and trailing scarves, purchased war-surplus Dakotas and earned a living by transporting troops overseas, reaching their peak of usefulness during the Berlin airlift. Thereafter, they diversified into the holiday market, and by 1952 BEA had started to complain of 'material diversion' from its routes through non-scheduled flights, a complaint it was to reiterate incessantly for nearly twenty years until it, in turn, set up its own charter subsidiary – BEA Airtours. While the scheduled carriers have been struggling to agree to ever more complex fare structures and devise more elaborate methods to boost their falling occupancy rates, the charter airlines seem a model of profitable expansion and efficient business. The key to the success of the charter operation is that the operator can choose where he will fly from and to, and when he will fly. He can thus choose a route and a timetable which will give him the highest possible load factor. This in turn enables him to offer lower prices than the scheduled operator who is denied these vital choices. Further economies are possible through bulk sales to a tour operator or affinity group thus avoiding expensive direct handling with individual members of the public. As an example of the economies which are possible, between 1963 and 1971, the peak season seat rate for a tour operator for a return flight between the UK and Palma has dropped 20 per cent in money terms.[29] Since inflation eroded the value of money by about 35 per cent this represents a real reduction of about 27 per cent. (There was also an improvement of quality as jet aircraft replaced the old turbo-props.) These economies are the result of better occupancy rates, a longer season, larger aircraft, reduced margins and greater efficiency. The introduction of 400-seater aircraft may bring further economies though these could be outweighed by restrictions on night flying.

This formula has been enormously successful; between April and October 1961, 295,000 Britons travelled abroad on inclusive tour charters. The comparable figures for 1970 were 2,143,000. This tenfold growth must be compared with the mere doubling of passengers carried on scheduled services by BEA and BOAC over the same period. 97 per cent of the traffic between Spain and Scandinavia in 1971 went by charter, and most scheduled services have now been withdrawn.[30]

There are only a dozen large airlines in the world specializing in charter business – large in this instance meaning carrying over 1 million passengers per year. Most of these twelve are based in North America or Western Europe, and some of them are in fact owned by scheduled airlines. BEA owns Airtours (which is relatively small), Lufthansa in Germany owns Condor, Iberia owns Aviaco in Spain and Alitalia owns SAM in Italy. As with other sections of the industry there is the usual pattern of vertical integration. BOAC, QANTAS and Air India are all setting up non-IATA subsidiaries. Britannia Airways is owned by Thomson Travel Holidays. Another charter airline, Court, is owned by Court Line which comes from the same stable as Clarksons, the tour operators. Sterling, a Danish charter airline, is also owned by a travel agency, Tjaeroborg Rejser. Air Canada is owned by Canadian Pacific – a government-owned travel conglomerate which controls thirty-six hotels, a hundred restaurants, a railway, a shipping company, a tour operator and a travellers cheque business.

As with other sections of the tourist industry, the future for the airlines is bright if they can overcome their tariff setting problems. Less than 1 per cent of the world's population has currently flown in an aeroplane so the growth potential is almost limitless.

On tariffs, it is unlikely that the present distinction between scheduled fares and charter fares will last much longer; there are no longer two distinct markets, one for charter flights and one for scheduled, so the public does not accept the distinction or indeed understand it. Problems of enforcibility are such that the authorities are likely to abandon it as soon as a convenient opportunity presents itself. So great is the problem of enforcibility that in 1972 the presidents and chairmen of more than sixty IATA airlines held a conference in Geneva to try to find a formula to halt the growing volume of malpractices, particularly 'fare discounting' which was losing member airlines some $200 million in revenue on the North Atlantic routes alone.[31] It would be much easier for everyone if such practices were made legal, particularly for IATA airlines, as they would then be able to compete on equal terms with charter airlines. A foretaste of the future in the airline industry was provided in the UK in 1972 when British Caledonian introduced the first low-fare walk-on air service between London and Scotland. No advance reservations were possible, but the fare was 43 per cent below the normal tariff and was even lower than the railfare. This gives an example of the fare cutting opportunities which are possible if the tariff structure is changed.

Aircraft

Civil aircraft manufacturers are also part of the tourist industry and depend on the continued growth of tourism for survival. Their role has been rather unkindly portrayed by Lord Beeching. 'The aircraft industry is a sort of Alice in Wonderland world, where subsidized engines are put in subsidized airframes to be operated by subsidized airlines, who don't want the wretched thing anyway.'[32]

Historically, civil aircraft have been able to benefit from research and development of military aircraft, and manufacturers were able to use the same production techniques. Civil aircraft and military aircraft are now parting company, and the military side is taking the government money with it. In 1970–71, the government gave the aeronautical industry £335 million. £247 million went on defence, and most of the balance went on Concorde. Concorde is the exception that proves the rule; while it is indeed the case that it is being built with public funds it is exceedingly doubtful whether £1,000 million of public funds would have been committed had the public and its elected representatives known that this is what the final commitment would be; and from this it follows that any further proposals for public finance for civil aircraft would be viewed with intense suspicion.

Civil aircraft manufacturers are therefore having to manage without the cushion of a military budget; nor are their problems eased by the development of aircraft technology. As the aircraft get bigger and more complicated, so the airlines tend to rationalize their purchasing and just buy one of a kind. In 1967, fifteen different types of airliner were on the market. In 1972, there were only five. As a result production runs are likely to be longer, but there is no room for more than two types of big aircraft, thus restricting the number of possible manufacturers. Already 55 per cent of the free-world's commercial aircraft are made by Boeing.[33] Thus only Boeing are building jumbo jets; only Lockheed and McDonnell Douglas are building wide-body Tri-jets and there is only one short-haul airbus, the A 300B.

As a result of this trend, there is a growing tendency towards international collaboration amongst aircraft manufacturers to spread the business and the risk. Thus the UK and France have joined together on Concorde. Germany and France are getting together on the A 300B airbus; and the UK, France and Germany are collaborating on the RB 199 engine. Boeing has linked up with Alitalia to produce a short take-off and landing aircraft. The cost of an aeroplane has risen from £300,000 for an early Viscount to £12 million for a jumbo jet and £23 million for a Concorde. The stakes are now so large that no one company – and sometimes no one country – can afford to go it alone with aircraft developments. If the number of airlines decreases through mergers and if the variety of aircraft manufactured decreases, the future of a very large industry would be in the hands of a few men in charge of the airlines. At this stage, the politicians may well have to step in to avoid too much power accruing to too few people.

Since the introduction of the Comet in the early 1950s, jets have been replacing propeller-driven aircraft. In 1966, 27 per cent of the world's aircraft were jets; by 1971, over half were jets. However, aircraft have a very long life; 300 out of the 483 Viscounts, first introduced in 1950, were still in operation in 1972. Currently, the jumbo jet – the Boeing 747 – is the industry's most conspicuous response to the tourist boom. Total production is likely to be over 1,000 and the existing capacity of about 362 passengers can be increased to 1,000 by extending the upper deck bubble along the full length of the hull. In this form, the aircraft should be capable of handling growth up to the middle of the next decade before it is replaced by a faster and quieter vehicle.

Aircraft noise is another problem which the manufacturers are having to face. One quarter of the aircraft movements at Heathrow cause half the noise, and the Boeing 707 which exceeds the new regulation noise levels will be with us for another fifteen years. It is not a problem which can be solved overnight, and the growth in long-haul traffic may make the problem more difficult to solve. Long-haul aircraft have to be large to carry sufficient passengers and fuel to make the journey profitable. This means bigger and, to date, noisier engines. Like so many other problems of the industry, it can be solved by money, and stiffer legislation is likely to compel the manufacturer to find solutions, albeit expensive ones.

Shipping

Fortunately for the companies concerned, the decline of shipping as a means of transporting individuals has coincided with the emergence of cruising as a popular form of holiday. With appropriate modifications, many of the world's better known liners are now floating hotels drifting from one sun-bathed pleasure resort to another. In 1971, some 500,000 UK citizens went on a cruise, three quarters of them going to the cruising area by aeroplane on an increasingly popular 'fly-cruise'.

Demand for cruises is clearly buoyant, and shipping companies are still finding it a profitable market to operate in. The most popular areas appear to be the Caribbean and Greek islands, where a number of different destinations are within commuting distance of each other in a more temperate part of the world. The Greek shipping lines tend to offer the cheapest fares as their labour is underpaid by Western standards and is prepared to undertake a multiplicity of duties, a practice shunned by the unions. There are, however, a number of clouds on the horizon; cruising is labour intensive and some 65 per cent of operating costs are attributable to wages. With one crew member to 2·1 passengers on some ships, the impact of rising wages on fares is immediate and inevitable. While the present generation of ships can probably be run profitably, there is a marked reluctance to invest in new purpose-built cruise ships. One of the latest ones, the Cunard Adventurer, cost £12 million to build in 1971 or more than £12,000 per berth. This is much more than it costs to provide a hotel bed in central London which can be let at £20 per night and unlike a hotel, a ship does not appreciate in value. It is most unlikely that the European cruise market can bear the high tariffs involved in building ships at today's costs and staffing them with today's labour and for this reason a mass cruising market is unlikely to develop.

The shipping companies are well aware of this and they are either diversifying into the more profitable car-ferry or freight market or are moving into the more profitable sections of the holiday market. Cunard has acquired two tour operators – Sunair and Lunn-Poly – before in turn being acquired by Trafalgar House. Court Line, originally a shipping company, is now a travel conglomerate owning a Caribbean airline and 1,200 beds in the Caribbean islands. It is interesting to note that internationally agreed sea-fares are now under pressure in the same way as airfares are. Cunard has withdrawn from the Atlantic Steamship Passenger Conference and has started a fare cutting exercise. Cruising is unlikely to expand at a very fast rate, though there will always be a market for the more specialized cruises.

Hotels

One of the themes of this chapter is that the component sections of the tourist industry have not been growing at mutually com-patible rates, and that an overall framework, or tourist plan, is needed to avoid the resultant dangers of unbalanced growth.

This theme is well illustrated by the accommodation industry, particularly in the UK; the world airlines are arranging their tariff structures in such a way that a sizeable increase in passengers can now be expected from the lower-income groups, and in par-ticular from the young. Yet the hotels being built to accommodate this growth are manifestly beyond the means of these travellers of the future. A tourist who is persuaded to visit London from the USA by a reduction in the return airfare to £40 – as opposed to £120 – is not the sort of tourist who will spend £12 per night for his accommodation. Yet this is the price range of most of the hotels being built to cater for the new traffic generated by lower fares. In the words of the City of Westminster Development Plan, 'All new purpose-built accommodation in the City [of Westminster] appears to be in the high-price category.'[34]

Because of the absence of an overall strategy, there is therefore a danger of over-capacity in the higher-priced hotels and under-capacity in the lower-priced hotels; and the likelihood of no camping sites anywhere near the centre of the capital for younger visitors. Christian Action summed up the problem well in their publication 'Unwanted Visitors', 'The number of hostel beds has remained fairly static despite the fact that hard-up tourists are arriving in increasing numbers. One half of our tourists are under 30. For them the situation was, and is, desperate.'[35]

The accommodation industry also provides evidence for the

hypothesis that a country should relate the marketing effort devoted to promoting its tourist industry to the industry's capacity to absorb tourists. Again, Christian Action, with religious self-restraint, has identified the problem, 'The situation was not helped by the British Tourist Authority which has been sending brochures claiming that accommodation could be obtained for 30p per night. By March 1970, one 120-bed hostel had turned down 34,184 applications for beds . . . some hostels are booked up for the next five years.'

Accommodation is a critical ingredient in the tourist cake; if there is a discrepancy, qualitatively or quantitatively, between what is provided and what is needed, there is inevitably confusion, ill-feeling and waste of resources. In the 1960s, the world supply of hotel rooms grew at about 6 per cent per annum; to keep pace with growing demand for travel, it should have grown at about 10 per cent.

It is also accommodation, more than any other component, which dictates the sort of tourist industry a country can expect. For example, the hotels in France and Italy developed a long time ago and in the 1950s and 1960s the hotel industry in those countries was too deeply entrenched to respond to the needs of the package tour operators. In Spain, however, the industry did not develop so early and was therefore better able to respond to today's needs of the lower income traveller.

In examining the accommodation industry a convenient starting point is to look at the changing pattern of ownership within the industry and to examine the complex industrial alliances which are beginning to emerge. Historically, the U K hotel industry has been composed of a large number of independent units, and this accounted for the relatively fragmented nature of the industry up to the middle of this century. Indeed, about 80 per cent of the units are still independently owned and this has meant that a large proportion of the industry is under-capitalized and excessively labour intensive. However, since the Second World War, a number of factors have been at work which have combined to concentrate ownership of the country's hotels into fewer hands.

Firstly, many independent units were acquired by the aggressive hotel companies started after the war. Perhaps the best known of these is Grand Metropolitan Hotels, which now own twenty hotels in London, most of which were bought rather than built. Other large groups, such as Trust Houses and Strand Hotels (the hotel subsidiary of J. Lyons) have also acquired independent units and smaller companies, further concentrating ownership. 75 per cent of the 288 London hotels in the 1968 Hotels Survey were group affiliated.[36]

Secondly, the economics of hotel operation are now such that larger groups have a distinct advantage over smaller ones. Centralized purchasing schemes and the need to have access to substantial sums of money to build the larger hotel units of today give the bigger group the edge. They can afford the best management and marketing techniques and can buy expensive computer terminals for today's reservation systems. Thirdly, many independent units have simply disappeared; some have been the victims of redevelopment schemes; others, through their location, have been better suited to rented accommodation or offices and have been converted.

Since the war, there has therefore been a process of horizontal integration, as independent units became parts of larger groups, and these larger groups have in turn become responsible for building the newer and bigger hotels. Recently, this process of horizontal integration has been complemented by one of vertical integration. Companies operating in the transport and leisure fields have extended their interests to include accommodation; at the same time, the 'traditional' hotel companies have been following the same logic, and building up their own interests in businesses related to, but outside the accommodation industry, e.g. brewing, catering and travel.

The most conspicuous of the newcomers to the hotel industry are the airlines; because they have noticed the imbalance mentioned at the beginning of the chapter – a shortage of cheaper accommodation to match the cheaper seats on their aircraft – and have recognized it as a potential threat to their ability to expand, they have invested in hotels all over the world. Although PanAm started Intercontinental Hotels in the 1940s it was not until the 1960s that the airlines became a force to be reckoned with in the accommodation industry. Their objects in doing this are summarized by Mr Gilbert Lee, Chairman of BOAC Associated Companies, 'We do not plan to go into the hotel business in a big way. We intend to leave this to the experts in this direction. But what we are keen to provide is an economical type of hotel in which we shall invest money to provide for passengers on our routes where we consider there is a need.' Evidence of this keenness is BOAC's financial assistance to the YMCA, under which BOAC has access to a number of rooms in two of YMCA's current developments. At the plusher end of the market, BOAC has a stake in game lodges and hotels in East Africa through a Swiss based company run by His Highness the Aga Khan.

If removing a potential bottleneck to expansion is one motive for the airlines' involvement, another one is to see that the benefits of cheaper flying are not lost to the travelling public by the accommodation industry increasing its tariffs as fast as the airlines lower theirs. By integrating vertically in this way, the airlines can ensure that the economies inherent in larger planes and higher load factors are passed right down the line to the customer, and not siphoned off *en route* by other component industries.

A third motive is to increase sales outlets. The airlines are not in the hotel business simply to sell beds to their passengers; they can also sell their air tickets to their guests. This is more easily done when the hotel is controlled by the airline in question and the visitor is not confused by the suggestion of alternative airlines.

The airlines also have the support facilities to move into the hotel business – in particular their sophisticated reservation systems. Originally designed for air passengers, they are equally applicable to hotel guests, and through its Boadicea reservation system, BOAC will shortly be selling hotel beds at the same time as it sells air tickets. BOAC also has a 10 per cent stake in Citel, the European hotel booking scheme. The airlines will thus have considerable influence in deciding where people will stay, and it would be unreasonable to expect them not to use this influence to benefit their own hotels.

Not only do the individual airlines have their own hotel companies, or joint ventures with other hotel companies, they also cooperate with each other to remove threats to their collective business. The European Hotel Consortium is such a collaborative exercise between five major European airlines and five European banks to build medium-priced hotels in European cities faced with a shortage. The hotels are actually operated by hotel companies – Grand Metropolitan Hotels being the partner in London and Paris. BOAC and PanAm, implacable enemies over the North Atlantic, are collectively involved in the development of the Portman Hotel in London. Joint ventures with hotel companies are probably more common; before its merger with Trust Houses, Fortes operated seven hotels with BEA – principally at airports – and three with BOAC.

One side effect of airline involvement in hotels has been the increase in size of hotels; as the capacity of aircraft has increased, and as the tendency to travel on inclusive tours has similarly increased, so it has become convenient, if not essential, to equate the capacity of the hotels the passengers are destined for with the capacity of the planes carrying them. It is no coincidence that the largest hotel in London – the Tara Hotel in Kensington – is part owned by Aer Lingus.

After the airlines, perhaps the most significant new arrivals are the breweries. In the days of the old coaching inns, some brewers were accustomed to accommodating the traveller and they have recently been reviving this aspect of their business.

They have been doing this for two main reasons; firstly, to provide more tied outlets for the sale of their beer and other liquor, and secondly to maximize the value of their properties – which are often ideally located, being large pubs on the main roads with some spare land. The breweries are acutely conscious that the return they are making on their properties is in some cases as low as 2 or 3 per cent and hotel development can increase this.

If these are the main motives, the opportunity has been provided by the rationalization of the brewing industry itself, which has placed it in a stronger position to enter the hotel market. Between 1960 and 1970, the number of independent brewers dropped from 250 to 100, and seven brewers now account for 75 per cent of the UK's output of beer. The resources, both financial and management, of the brewing industry are now concentrated enough for it to make an impact on the accommodation industry;

all the big UK brewers are now hotel owners. Courage own 25 Anchor Hotels, Bass Charrington have 80 Crest Hotels and 2,000 rooms and are now moving into the motel market. By 1979 they will have 16 motels and over 1,100 motel rooms; Vaux are building hotels and motels in the North of England and in Scotland; the hotel subsidiary of Allied Breweries – Ind Coope Hotels Ltd – has 46 hotels with 2,100 bedrooms, and plans to build 400 more rooms. Allied Breweries announced in their 1970 Annual Report that 'the policy of adding letting bedrooms and catering facilities to suitable houses has continued'. Whitbread have 70 hotels, and a partnership with Trafalgar House Investments – themselves in the hotel business – for the purpose of developing Whitbread properties. Watneys have 40 hotels and are also building motels 100 miles from each other to catch the itinerant and thirsty motorist.

The oil companies have also been moving into the hotel industry recently; their motives are similar to those of the brewers and the airlines. Firstly, the absence of suitable hotels for the motorist to stay in, particularly in Europe, may result in loss of business to other modes of transport which are less extravagant in their consumption of petroleum products. Secondly, guests at their hotels and motels are captive customers for the sale of petrol and ancillary motoring goods and services.

Esso have nearly fifty hotels and motels in Western Europe; Gulf Oil Corporation have joined with PanAm and put up £2 million each to build a motel chain in Europe; and Burmah Oil is considering a scheme involving joint development of hotels with Grand Metropolitan. The logic of the former merger is that Gulf's skills in servicing the motorist's needs, and PanAm's skills in looking after the traveller, can usefully be pooled. 'Within five years, the motorist will be able to drive through Europe confident that he can find a consistent quality of accommodation available to him,' in the words of the managing director of the joint project. British Petroleum is aiming rather lower; it has a stake in a Turkish company providing camping and caravan sites.

Other interests are also moving into the hotel business. The holiday camps, for instance, have discovered that their loyal customers are now abandoning the older UK camps for sunnier climes in Europe. They are therefore following them; Warners have moved into the package tour business, and own the Hotel Kontiki at Arenal, Majorca. Pontins own hotels in Cala Masquida, Majorca and in Sardinia (the Pineta Beach). Butlins have hotels in the UK at traditional places such as Brighton, Blackpool and Margate, but have a toe in the overseas market by owning a travel agency. The Lex Service Group – originally garage proprietors – are building hotels at Heathrow, Gatwick and Stratford, as they widen the range of services they offer the travelling public. Ladbrokes – the bookies – and also the Playboy Club are building hotels with perhaps less industrial logic.

Overseas, other industries are similarly moving into the accommodation industry. The National Bank of Greece controls Astir, the leading tourist hotel company in that country. In Yugoslavia, agricultural interests are moving in; Beograd, the principal farming combine, is investing in a chain of quality hotels, holiday centres and restaurants in order to market agricultural produce directly to the tourist industry. In France, Club Méditerranée is building a hotel in Paris.

As fast as other companies move into the hotel market, the traditional hotel companies are lessening their dependence on hotels by expanding elsewhere. Their main advantage in the hotel market is that they own the best sites and have developed them at yesterday's costs. Further expansion in hotels means developing inferior sites at today's costs, and thus throwing away their inbuilt competitive advantage. Insofar as they are extending their hotel interests, it is usually in such a way as not to be manoeuvred into this position – thus they buy existing hotels, often overseas. Fortes have recently bought three prestige hotels in central Paris, Grand Metropolitan have bought the Royal Manhattan in New York; alternatively, they exchange shares in other hotel companies, e.g. Trust Houses and Travelodge (Australia) Ltd. In the recent scramble for new sites in London, the older companies have been noticeably absent.

This philosophy is summed up in the Annual Report of Grand Metropolitan Hotels in April 1971, when the chairman referred to a 'policy of diversification into allied activities, such as the dairy and leisure industries. The company has taken steps to ensure future growth and profitability without having to rely entirely upon a continuing increase in the tourist business.'

By 1970, hotels only accounted for a third of G M H's turnover. With the acquisition of Truman's and Watney's Breweries, and as a result of further diversification, hotel management now provides only 18·5 per cent of group profits. The company now has a sizeable stake in the processing and distribution of milk and milk products, including 50 per cent of the U K yoghurt market, through the acquisition of Express Dairies. It runs 800 canteens and staff restaurants in the U K through two catering subsidiaries, and owns 500 steak houses and restaurants, mostly through the Chef and Brewer and Berni Inns subsidiaries. It is in the dancing, ice-skating and Miss World business through Mecca; in gaming through City Tote, and even in merchant banking through Robert Fraser and Partners. And of course, it is now a force to be reckoned with in the brewing industry through Trumans, which owns 1,000 pubs and a brand new brewery; and through Watneys, which has added 6,100 pubs in the U K, 5,100 on the continent, 1,200 off-licences and 31 hotels and motels.

In addition to a partnership with the European Hotel Consortium referred to earlier, the company has an arrangement with British Rail to promote 'mini-holidays', which brought the group 50,000 winter visitors in 1970. The group also has extensive interests in hotels overseas, owning hotels in Amsterdam, Brussels, Cannes, Madrid, Monte Carlo and Paris.

Trust Houses – another large 'traditional' hotel group is similarly diversifying out of hotels; in 1967, before the merger with Fortes, the Chairman said in the Annual Report: 'After studying all the aspects of the matter, we have felt compelled to decide that the (future hotel development programme) must be sharply curtailed.' Even then, hotels were accounting for under 50 per cent of revenue. In September 1971, the merged group scrapped plans for a £35 million motel chain in Europe. The company has diversified into industrial catering through Gardener Merchants, the largest industrial catering organization in the U K which has a kitchen which can produce 10,000 meals a day; it has diversified into travel, by owning a tour operator and travel agent – Allways Travel Service – which offers package holidays to some of the group's hotels overseas. It has diversified into the leisure field, and amongst other interests owns Eastbourne Pier and runs the amusement concessions at Madame Tussaud's. After the merger with Fortes, which made the group one of the three largest hotel and catering groups in the world, its interests in catering, travel and leisure were considerably extended, Fortes owning Hickie Borman and Grant, Milbanke Travel and other travel companies. Together they own 215 hotels and 18,200 rooms in the UK and overseas.

Other traditional hotel companies have diversified in different ways; Kensington Palace Hotel has moved into the security business through Securicor. At first sight, the industrial logic is difficult to perceive, but it is there. Hotels require a large amount of capital, and they generate a relatively small cash flow. To balance this, KPH required a business that did not need a large amount of capital but had a large cash flow. The security business answers this description and accounts for about 95 per cent of the group's turnover and 10 per cent of the fixed assets. This logic has recently been strengthened by the group's plans to build high security lorry parks and 'lotels' for the drivers.

There are exceptions to most rules; while most of the 'traditional' hotel companies are effectively diluting their hotel interests by diversifying out, some of the newer companies are expanding very fast. These are the international hotel companies, particularly Holiday Inns. This company builds a new hotel room every 20 minutes, and a new hotel every 52 hours. In July 1972, it ran 1,423 hotels and has plans to build 10 hotels in the UK in each of the next five years.

There are several important implications from this analysis of the hotel industry; the emergence of travel conglomerates and the interest in hotels shown by international airlines and international oil companies means that ownership of the newer and larger hotels is often in the hands of companies domiciled outside the country where the hotel is built. This affects the validity of the balance of payments argument frequently adduced for supporting the tourist industry. Secondly, there are signs that there is a 10-year cycle in the hotel industry, and it may be that this is related to the 10-year cycle in the airline industry. The evidence for this hotel cycle is somewhat tentative; but in Jamaica in the late 1950s and early 1960s there was a hotel building boom; this was followed by a period of excess capacity up to 1967. In 1971–2 another boom started and accommodation capacity is likely to double in three to four years. This will almost certainly lead to another period of excess capacity and so the cycle continues. If this analysis were correct, then London is due for another building boom at the end of the decade. More important, if hotel building is not a continuous process which can be monitored and adjusted, then the periods of intense activity must be controlled so that problems are not caused in other sections of the tourist industry. Further, it should be compatible with other 10-year cycles, particularly that of investment in aircraft. The implications of continuing hotel development are analysed in subsequent chapters.

Car-Rental

The car-rental business is an important part of the UK tourist industry, and one which is growing fast. It provides an example of how business and profits generated by tourism to the UK are increasingly going to non-UK firms; two of the three largest car-hire firms in the UK are American owned.

There are several reasons why the industry is growing fast; not only are its fortunes closely linked with the tourist industry – itself growing fast, but in addition it has benefited from the spread of car-ownership in the tourist generating countries. People whose lives at home are geared to the motor car are clearly more likely to hire one when they go abroad. The UK car hire firms enjoy an advantage over their continental rivals since the channel forms an inconvenient barrier for the cars of European motorists. Further, as lengths of stay have decreased, the economics have favoured car-hire rather than car-ferry. The development of a steady, if modest, programme of inter-city motorways and motels has encouraged the growth of motorized tourism, from which the car-hire firms have also benefited. Our custom of driving on the left-hand side of the road appears to have had little deterrent effect.

While it is growing fast, the car-hire industry exhibits many features of an undeveloped structure. There is an extremely large number of small operators, who account for over half the business. In this respect, the car-hire business is more like the hotel industry and travel agents, and less like the airlines. In common with the first two, there will probably be some tidying up over the next decade as the smaller firms get driven out of business or swallowed up by the larger ones, a process which will be expedited by the increasing popularity of computerized reservations, in-house credit cards and massive advertising campaigns.

As with other component parts of the tourist industry, there is a complex of interlocking relationships, as tour operators, airlines and railways buy their way in through vertical integration; even the National Coal Board has an interest through its computer-based International Reservation System. This has access to 8,000 cars in 70 locations and can find the right one in 15 seconds. There are further complications as the car-hire firms diversify out. Auto-Meyer, one of Germany's biggest car-rental firms, has started its own charter airline, concentrating on carrying low-cost package tour groups organized by the smaller operators. The British firm, Budget Rent-a-Car, are diversifying sideways by starting Budget Rent-a-Boat.

The size of the UK car-rental industry is difficult to assess, but it has been estimated[37] that in 1971 there were about 50,000 rented cars on Britain's roads, generating an income of £40 million per annum. 40 per cent of these vehicles were accounted for by the Big Three – Hertz having 8,000, and Godfrey Davis and Avis about 6,000 each. Annual growth in revenue over the past three years has been of the order of 25 per cent. Size of fleet is a dubious measure as the well-managed operator will adjust his fleet size according to demand. Indeed, profits of the car-hire firms are sensitive to the level of second-hand car prices, and £5 difference in the selling price of second-hand cars can affect profits to the order of £25,000.

Fleet usage is of the order of 75 per cent – a high ratio which reflects the ability of the fleet operator to sell surplus cars at slack times of the year – an operation denied to the hotelier.

Godfrey Davis have links with British Rail and BEA. Since transport interchanges represent the ideal locations, these tie-ups make good commercial sense. The BEA passenger can book his car with his flight, and similar arrangements are available to the railway passenger. By the end of 1972, Davis had 220 outlets in the UK including kiosks at 73 railway stations, and were opening two new locations a week. They are diversifying overseas, and have purchased Holland's Rent-a-Car.

The future for the industry looks bright; while garages will be a major source of competition, the large firms have the edge in reliability, convenience and security. Their position will become more dominant, and the competition between them more intense. Connections with other components of the tourist industry are likely to develop – for example, more hotels will offer office space to car-hire firms on their premises, and tour operators will develop closer links as they sell mobile packaged holidays. A new source of competition could be the car manufacturers who are beginning to move into car-hire, and indeed inclusive tours. Citer, the inclusive holiday subsidiary of Citroën, is marketing twelve-day trans-Sahara tours from Algeria. These are based on a Citroën-built jeep driven by holiday-makers on a rota basis for 1,000 miles. In addition Citroën has extended its self-drive car rental network to the UK and Volkswagen operates a growing car-rental business through its dealers.

Tourist Attractions

In 1971, the British Tourist Authority estimated that 20 million visits were made to historic houses in the UK; roughly the same as the total gate for league soccer throughout the winter. About one quarter of these visits were accounted for by overseas visitors, and, at an average of 20p admission, this is a £6 million business. Some 809 properties are open to the public; some are government owned; others are owned by the National Trust and the rest are privately-owned.

In terms of attendance, the three most popular stately homes are Beaulieu, Longleat and Woburn. Beaulieu attracts about ½ million visitors per year, spending on average 75p each. Like other sections of the tourist industry, the owners of stately homes are diversifying into the leisure and entertainment business, and reducing their dependence on the buildings themselves. Beaulieu has a motor museum, and the other two have wild game in their parks, run by Chipperfields. There is a further trend towards diversification into funfairs and pop concerts.

Of the 140 historic houses run by the National Trust, 70 are run at a loss. It is indeed a sad commentary on the way we run our affairs that so little of the revenue generated by tourism is directed towards the maintenance and improvement of our tourist attractions. St Paul's Cathedral needs £3 million as a minimum amount to keep it going; the piers supporting the dome are apparently bending outwards. This money will probably be found, but the tourist industry has not so far appeared very often in the subscription list. Whereas admission to the Cathedral is now free, in the nineteenth century visitors had to pay half a crown to look round.

Most of the tourist attractions are concentrated in London, and this is the nub of the problem of the UK tourist industry. The Changing of the Guard, Westminster Abbey, St Pauls, Trafalgar Square, the Tower of London and the Houses of Parliament are the foundations of the tourist industry. It is at these places that congestion is at its worst.

The Changing of the Guard is attended, though not seen, by 15,000 people per day at the height of the tourist season. The numbers have been estimated to be increasing at an annual rate of 20 per cent.[38] Two hundred coaches arrive on some days, whereas there is only parking space for ninety-two of them. The column of traffic which the attraction generates is acknowledged to be a nuisance, coinciding with the end of the morning rush-hour and creating jams in the glue-pot which is central London. Suggestions that the number of performances might be increased or the location changed to a more appropriate venue – such as Horseguards Parade – are rewarded with gestures of stern impatience by the military authorities, who reply that their men are soldiers and not actors.

Westminster Abbey has its own problems; the authorities have been compelled to introduce entry charges for the Royal Chapels, and to adopt traffic management schemes elsewhere in the Abbey. There is a rigidly enforced one way system to avoid conflict, coupled with an effective 'no waiting' scheme to keep the traffic moving. Although it has been estimated that the environmental

capacity of the Abbey is 700 visitors, at 11 a.m. in July–August
1970, the crowds inside reached 3,000.[39]

It is possible to increase the capacity of these popular tourist
attractions by extending the opening hours and managing tourist
flows more efficiently. But this cannot be done indefinitely and the
tourist authorities must recognize that there is a point beyond
which further increases in tourist flows simply cannot be handled.
Their efforts to broaden the base of the tourist industry by widening
the range of tourist attractions has not yet succeeded and continued increases can only lead to queues and frustrations at those
attractions which every visitor wants to see.

Conclusions

The picture that emerges from this brief analysis is one of increasing domination by larger companies whose interests cross many
national frontiers. This trend has advantages and disadvantages:
on the one hand, it can lead to a more streamlined industry with
less fat in it by, for example, reducing the number of travel agents
and eliminating some of the smaller and less efficient tour operators. On the other hand, the growth in activity occasioned by these
companies can accentuate other structural imbalances which they
cannot rectify – deficient airports for example. Further, the traditional financial arguments for supporting tourism are, at best,
obscured and, at worst, eliminated by the takeover of national
tourism by international companies. The momentum of the larger
companies, in particular the airlines, is now such that any future
efforts to redirect or indeed restrain growth will be less likely to
succeed. Yet such efforts must be made. The need for an indicative
tourist plan, on a national and international basis, within which
the component parts of the industry can identify and fulfil their
own particular roles is the best, though not the easiest, solution to
the problems that are identified. Such a solution is developed in
subsequent chapters.

6 The Local Impact of Tourism

Information on tourism tends to be presented in national terms, and decisions on its development taken at a national level. Thus we know that 7·2 million visitors came to the UK in 1971, and that the British Tourist Authority is the body with overall responsibility for tourist promotion. Yet tourism is essentially a local phenomenon, tending to be concentrated in a very small percentage of the land area of a given country. The geographical concentration of UK tourism in London is a good example of this phenomenon, some 90 per cent of all overseas visitors spending some time in the capital, and 75 per cent of these never leaving it. Half the tourist nights spent in Holland are spent in Amsterdam; (yet only one visitor in twenty to Austria visits Vienna). It is therefore important to know the effect of national decisions, taken in the national interest, on the relatively few areas of a country affected by those decisions in order that possible conflicts of interest may be identified in advance, clarified and resolved.

It would of course be wrong to maintain that there is an inevitable conflict between the national interest, requiring a growth in tourist numbers for reasons analysed in the next chapter, and the interest of the tourist regions which have to absorb these numbers. Often, the best interests of the region and the nation coincide; but sometimes they do not and the region suffers as a result. The national benefits of tourism are easily quantified in terms of expenditure though, as the next chapter shows, they are often exaggerated. The regional and local disbenefits are less easily quantified, often underestimated and this side of the argument therefore goes by default.

The hypothesis expounded in this chapter is that there is a saturation level for tourism in a given locality or region and if that level is exceeded, the costs of tourism begin to outweigh the benefits. These saturation levels may be dictated by the availability of labour, the amount of land suitable for hotel development, the capacity of the roads or of the principal tourist attractions in the area. If a national policy for tourism is formulated without regard for these saturation levels – and there are signs that this is happening – then that policy is a bad one which should be revised.

The concept of saturation levels for tourism is not yet widely recognized, though it is easy to demonstrate. Tourism is a sequence of visits by various people to various destinations. If any one destination is considered in isolation, be it a beach, a restaurant, the Changing of the Guard or a beauty spot, there is a limit to the number of people that can visit it at any one time. The limit may be a physical one as at a restaurant where, quite simply, there is nowhere to sit; or a practical one, where visitors above a certain number cannot see anything, or are in such physical discomfort that it is not worth the effort. In some cases, it may be possible to increase the supply and postpone the achievement of saturation levels. For example, the Guard can be changed more often, Westminster Abbey and the Tower of London can be opened at night and more restaurants or hotels can be built. But, in the first three cases a saturation level will still eventually be reached; and in the last two one is simply increasing the number of possible destinations, which does not contradict the hypothesis that, for any given destination, there is a maximum number of tourists which it can accommodate.

The concept is equally valid, though less easy to demonstrate, at the next scale up where there is an aggregation of tourist attractions as in a city or region. It is less easy to demonstrate the validity of this concept at the regional level because the obvious physical limitations which characterize saturation levels at the individual tourist destinations are absent. This may explain why so little work has been done in this field. However, a growing number of tourists in a given locality can create problems in four main ways, and it is in these respects that one can justify the argument for local or regional saturation levels.

Firstly, the diversion of land to accommodating tourists denies the use of that land for other, often more urgent, purposes such as houses, schools and open space. Secondly, the growth of seasonal and low-paid employment needed to service the tourist industry can be a threat to the local employment structure. Thirdly, a steadily increasing tourist flow puts pressure on the general urban infrastructure – and particularly on the transport networks. Fourthly, due to a combination of the above factors, a stage is reached where the alienation of local inhabitants is inevitable. These four factors which together determine the saturation level for an area are examined in more detail.

Firstly, the diversion of land. This problem varies in intensity from area to area. Although it is at its most acute in capital cities and historic towns, and at its least acute at seaside resorts and the newer tourist regions, there are problems in the less densely populated areas of the world. At Serengeti and Ngorogoro Parks in Africa, there is a conflict between the needs of tourists and the needs of cattle and game; in Ethiopia, there is a conflict between the creation of the major tourist attraction of Awash National Park and the needs of the tribes currently living there. But the conflict of land use is at its worst in the capitals, where land is at a premium and there is pressure to use what there is to increase the quantity of open space, to reduce housing densities, to provide for urban motorways, to build new schools, universities, hospitals, to provide more and better offices and to meet a host of other urban needs. A continued and uncontrolled increase in tourist arrivals due to national promotion campaigns must prejudice the attainment of these regional objectives, and therefore reduce the quality of life as land, badly needed for other purposes, is acquired for hotels. A sensible land use policy for any area must represent a balance between the competing demands for that land; one such demand is for accommodation for overseas visitors, and it is right that such demand should be provided in accordance with a list of priorities which recognizes other needs. It is however quite wrong that an open-ended commitment to accommodate tourists should prejudice the fulfilment of these other needs. Hotels do have a genuine role to play in the local economy; they can make a town centre redevelopment outside the city centre itself a viable commercial proposition; they can be used to rehabilitate historic buildings which might otherwise fall down; they can infuse new life into an area which has become run-down and generate activity and prosperity for the local resident. This role needs to be identified in the context of regional or local needs, not dictated in pursuance of rigid national objectives. When that role has been identified, local government needs the powers to see that it is fulfilled.

This conflict of land use is visible in London. It has been calculated[1] that if all those who wish to visit London in July 1980 are to be accommodated, London needs 220,000 more hotel beds than it had in 1970. This would take about one square mile of land. Since London has already been shown[2] to be short of 5,000 acres of housing land if it is to accomplish its 1980 house building target, continuing diversion of land to hotels can only aggravate an already very serious situation. Yet the Greater London Council is unable to influence the promotional activity of the British Tourist Authority which is stoking up tourist demand with posters of Beefeaters and Carnaby Street in the four corners of the world.

The roots of this problem are economic ones. Given the high prices which visitors are prepared to pay to stay in hotels, and the relatively low rents which many Londoners pay under the fair rent scheme, a developer will naturally build rooms to rent to visitors i.e. hotels, rather than rooms to rent to Londoners, i.e. flats. He will certainly continue to do so until rents are decontrolled, or hotel tariffs are regulated; and he might well continue to do so thereafter as a differential would probably still exist. There is also a financial incentive for the local authority to permit hotel development, which makes a welcome contribution to the rate fund, rather than public housing, which is a drain on it. The same financial incentives persuade owners of flats to convert them to hotel use, and existing legislation is inadequate to cope with this loss. Westminster City Council has quantified this loss as follows:

The development of hotels through conversions has been largely at the expense of residential accommodation, ranging from dwelling houses, flats and bedsitters through to rooming houses and boarding-houses. Between the beginning of 1965 and May 1971, permission was given for 4,459 bedspaces through conversions, representing a potential loss of some 1,240 homes.[3]

Tourism therefore poses a threat to local and regional planning where there is an open-ended commitment to provide land to accommodate visitors and where this commitment prejudices the attainment of other more important objectives. Saturation levels are reached in this respect when land allocated to hotels could produce a greater social benefit if it were allocated to some other use.

The second saturation level concerns employment; if a town or an area becomes too dependent on the tourist industry, it can adversely affect its employment structure. The broader economic implications of a growing proportion of the labour force being engaged in the tourist industry are analysed more fully in the next chapter; suffice it to say that the conclusions apply with greater validity to the tourist region – namely that the lower productivity potential of work in the tourist industry can have a depressing effect on regional economic growth. The effect is of course more pronounced at the regional level since the concentration in this type of employment is greater. The point is well made in the Greater London Council's consultative document 'Tourism and Hotels in London':

Employees in hotels are among London's lowest-paid workers, even taking into account payments in kind. The Department of Employment and Productivity Earnings Survey shows this quite clearly. In 1970, for example, the survey showed that male manual workers in the hotel and catering industry had average earnings only 67 per cent of the average for Greater London, 71 per cent of the average for Great Britain and 87 per cent of the average for all the Miscellaneous Services (e.g. in laundries, cinemas, motor repairing). Staff turnover is very high in London hotels, further suggesting the present low status and un-attractive nature of hotel work, which is characterised by relatively low proportions of managerial, skilled and semi-skilled jobs.[4]

The City of Westminster also highlights this problem:

Employment in the hotel industry is characterised by its largely seasonal nature, a high proportion of low-skilled low-paid workers, a high proportion of women employees, and a high proportion of part-time, student and unofficial family labour in the peak-summer season... Staff turnover in London's hotel industry is very high. This is due to low wages, long hours, evening and weekend work, lack of living-in facilities and often poor working conditions which have given employment in the hotel industry a low status.[5]

Taking the example of London a stage further, an extra 220,000 hotel beds over a decade may need an extra 100,000 hotel workers, and an equally large increase in other service labour in restaurants, night-clubs, boats, dry-cleaners etc. The job opportunities so created are often those resisted by planning authorities on strategic grounds, because they are unskilled, seasonal and badly paid with little promotion prospects.

It is indeed likely that less labour will be needed in the future to service a given number of tourists; changes in management techniques, the growth of hotel chains, the increasing size of the newly-built hotels and the lower levels of service accepted by tomorrow's visitors may reduce employment in hotels. The statistics on this are however slightly misleading; as traditional hotel services are eliminated or contracted out, so the hotel labour force indeed declines. But this decline is compensated for by increases in the service industries concerned, such as catering, dry-cleaning and hairdressing; the work still has to be done.

There are other less obvious side-effects; if the tourist industry is seasonal, labour may be imported from other parts of the country or from overseas to increase the labour supply. A new 125 room Holiday Inn hotel in the Caribbean needed 200 staff to operate it. Only 60 were available locally, so nearly three quarters of the staff had to be imported. They then had to be housed, and this added to the demand for land for housing mentioned earlier. Further, staff employed in hotels, restaurants, night-clubs and other tourist attractions often start and stop work when there is no public transport. This effectively means that many of them have to be housed right in the centre of the city, where there is nearly always a shortage of low-priced accommodation. This can also add to the burden on the rates if they are housed in high-cost low-rent public housing. Only 19 per cent of employees in London's hotels are currently accommodated by their employers.[6] It has been calculated that, in Hawaii, the cost to the public purse of importing an immigrant family of four can be as much as $3,041.[7]

In some countries, where the imported labour is of a different colour, race or creed to the resident labour force, there can be considerable political tension. Further, wages are frequently lost to the area if they are remitted home. The dangers deriving from the labour requirements of the tourist industry were well described in a supplement on The Cayman Islands.

> It would be relatively easy for the Government to authorise the entry of all the staff required. . . but this means an addition to the already very large expatriate population since there are some 2,000 foreigners working in the Islands (total population 10,000). In addition, the number of tourists is more than double the number of inhabitants. This could have an adverse effect on society and on the attitude the people have towards tourists and tourism in general. Government would do well to move ahead with caution so as to be sure that the society and economy can cope with each step as it is taken.[8]

In this context one can say that saturation levels have been reached when the unfavourable consequences of further growth in employment to service the tourist industry outweigh the benefits.

The third saturation level concerns the pressure on transport and general infrastructure, such as water supply, sewers, telephones, taxi services, electricity, police services, air terminals, etc. As with the problem of land use, it is mainly confined to the tourist cities rather than the newer tourist destinations where it is easier to plan in advance for the tourist inflow.

The problem in the cities arises in part from bad planning – in that much of the excess pressure was predictable had the planners looked far enough ahead; and in part from the absence of a tourist policy which relates the capacity of the city – even correctly planned – to its marketing overseas. So far as inadequate planning for tourism is concerned, the structure of local government is largely to blame; the management of the cities is run on behalf of the residents by elected city councils or their equivalents. They naturally equate the needs of the city with the needs of the city's residents and would suffer electoral embarrassment were they to do otherwise. The needs of the visitor to the city tend to be ignored as he has no vote and as a result there are inadequate or inappropriate facilities for him.

A frank admission of this has been made by the City of Westminster.

> The sudden increase in demand for hotel development created pressures on land which had not been envisaged in the initial develop-

ment plan. . . Policy guidelines have stemmed from consideration of specific problems which have arisen from time to time rather than from a comprehensive appraisal of the needs of tourism and hotel development.[9]

In addition, there is a regrettable tendency to plan ahead on the basis of forecasts of the future resident population and on the basis of surveys of their behaviour. Thus a survey on the recreational needs of London excluded the recreational needs of visitors to London. Forecasts of shopping requirements, bus journeys – even of water consumption – are often made on the basis of visitors being an insignificant consideration. Inadequate planning for tourism is therefore partly to blame for pressure on infrastructure and for saturation levels being reached.

The second reason is the absence of a tourist policy relating the marketing of a city or region to its capacity to absorb tourists. Excessive marketing may not be the fault of the city itself but of national tourist authorities, hotel groups, airlines and conference organizers. Whatever the cause, there is a limit, quite simply, to the number of people the infrastructure of a city can support without living conditions deteriorating; this limit may be the amount of open space, the capacity of the underground system, the width of the pavements in the shopping centres, the size of the popular department stores, the capacity of the sewage plant – all of these impose a limit on the population that can be decently supported and none of them can be quickly or cheaply extended. The existence of this particular saturation level has been acknowledged by the City of Westminster.

In the peak summer months the large volumes of visitors in the City are causing increased pedestrian and vehicular congestion, and although a high level of activity is compatible with the City's role as the showpiece of London, any level of activity over and above the City's capacity to handle it is likely to cause serious environmental deterioration.[10]

To overcome these problems, a recent study[11] has suggested that one tourist for every fifty residents is a desirable target, with a maximum of three tourists for fifty residents in some areas.

Traffic congestion is often the first saturation point to be reached and because of the way tourism is developing, the traffic congestion which it generates will probably get worse in the cities. Currently some 25 per cent of overseas visitors to London go on a coach tour, but the greater the proportion of visitors that arrive on organized tours arranged by the airlines, inclusive tour operators, affinity-groups or conference organizers, the longer will be the queue of buses proceeding from one tourist attraction to the next. Independent travellers tend to use public transport or to walk, and thus present less of a problem. The growing popularity of inclusive tours, the tendency for hotel development to take place outside central London and the shortening length of stay are all factors which point to a growth in coach traffic. It has been estimated[12] that the volume of coach traffic in London could increase by a factor of three between 1970 and 1975. Since the situation is already serious in the peak summer months with intense congestion at the air terminals, larger hotels and the popular tourist attractions, saturation in this particular respect has been reached and further growth must be discouraged.

Other services are also under pressure. The police, for example, have to devote much manpower to controlling crowds at the popular tourist attractions in the peak of the season; and at night, in London, they patrol the parks distributing leaflets from the London Tourist Board telling the incumbents where they can find cheap accommodation in more appropriate surroundings. Traffic wardens also spend a disproportionate amount of time on offenders driving hired cars, unfamiliar with or contemptuous of local parking regulations.

The problem is aggravated because tourists are more intensive users of sections of the urban infrastructure than residents (hospitals and schools excepted), and because their geographical distribution is less even. They travel more, shop more, visit more museums - even have more baths. They thus accelerate the attainment of saturation levels in the cities or require a proportionately higher amount of investment. Figures for London are not available, but in some instances the cost of providing the infrastructure for the tourist industry is twice as great as the cost of building the accommodation itself.[13]

This type of saturation level can be defined in terms familiar to traffic engineers; it is reached when the benefits to the last visitor to arrive in a locality are exceeded by the disbenefits to those who are already there.

Finally, but not least important, the interaction of the preceding three factors can lead to a psychological saturation level in the local residents, and to the loss of their goodwill towards tourists. It is a fact, regrettable perhaps, that tourists and the hotels in which they are accommodated are becoming less and less popular in the more attractive tourist destinations, and the natives are becoming restless.

In simple terms, more people means more sharing, and increasingly the locals are having to compete with visitors for a finite supply of services; it becomes more difficult for them to go to the theatre and opera; harder to find an empty telephone kiosk; takes longer to make a telephone call abroad; they have to wait longer to get served in the shops and to find a taxi: it takes longer to get from A to B as the road has to be shared with more and more people.

More people means not only more sharing; it means living at higher densities; not just at home but on the way to work, in the park, in the shops. Psychologists have been at pains to show, through expensive experiments performed on rats which they assure us are equally valid for humans, that animals become aggressive and neurotic if they are forced to live at higher densities. A high tourist flow increases by a substantial amount the density of persons per acre in many parts of the world, and while one would not wish to exaggerate the effect of this, it is clearly something to watch in view of the concerted effort everywhere in the world to reduce high density living.[14]

It is worth examining in some detail specific grievances which can lead to this psychological saturation level. The location of hotels is an obvious one. A good location for a hotel in a tourist city is near the public transport network – preferably an interchange thereof – with good access to major roads, not too far from the centre, and with a good range of shops, restaurants, open space and entertainment. Unfortunately, these locational characteristics are also sought after by local residents, who are thus already well-established in these sorts of areas in London, such as Mayfair,

Holland Park and Knightsbridge. The residents therefore resent the subsequent intrusion of hotels, and since they are usually articulate and well-represented, their views are given a wide audience.

Their objections to hotels have some force; hotels generate a considerable flow of traffic at times of day and night which may be convenient for the airlines, but which are less so for those living nearby. Those hotels which incorporate night-clubs or casinos compound the offence.

The architecture of hotels is another source of irritation locally. 'The new hotels, which will last two generations, and took perhaps two years to build, all look as if they had taken about two hours to design . . . It seems likely that the hotels of 1969–1973 would be recognized as a very undesirable accretion to our architectural heritage.'[15] To be profitable, hotels must be large and tall. They therefore tend to dominate the area in which they are built, and if they are not beautiful, this can have the effect of downgrading an area. Since the demand is now predominantly for medium-priced hotels, economics may aggravate this particular objection. Further, the dominance of hotels in a particular area can change the range of shops in that area and affect prices disadvantageously for the resident in those shops that remain. Small tradesmen like shoe-repairers are bought out by boutiques, high-priced restaurants, night-clubs and souvenir shops, none of which may be patronized by the discriminating resident. This transformation in the distribution pattern can occur in areas where there are no hotels – such as the Kings Road, London – if it is sufficiently well-known as a tourist attraction. While hotels are not the cause in these instances, visitors clearly are, and the local resident who wants to buy a toothbrush often has a very long way to walk. This phenomenon, in many ways the obverse of planning blight, can have the same effect of dissolving a local community, and there are now signs of community action groups launching anti-hotel campaigns. The first pamphlet circulated by Street Aid, a radical community action group operating in the Covent Garden area, had a section on tourism.

The minority interests who benefit are those with the capital to build the Hiltons and use them; the losers are the displaced local population and the rest of us who have to suffer the new townscapes and other disbenefits which certain tourists bring with them, and which local councils, planners and architects rationalise as necessary.

The sins which the hotel industry has committed against local residents are well summarized by the City of Westminster:

The major clusters of converted hotels are situated in primarily residential areas and are within designated conservation areas. The level of hotel activity in these areas has led to considerable loss of amenity to remaining long-term residents, through vehicular obstruction, high traffic flows, lack of parking space because of competition from hotel guests and staff, and late-night activity and noise caused by hotels themselves and by associated uses such as restaurants and clubs. In many cases the use has a greater adverse impact on the environment than the visual effect of the hotel buildings.[16]

Putting hotels on one side, the tourist industry can offend local inhabitants in other ways. Its growth has made gaming casinos more profitable, and they are increasing in number in the popular tourist destinations. While most are doubtless well-run establishments meeting a real, though regrettable, need, others are used for less innocent purposes and have brought the industry into disrepute. In particular, the owners of some establishments in the UK have caused the Home Office concern. Outside the UK, in tourist areas where the main appeal is gambling, strip-shows and brothels, there is a straight conflict between the economic advantages of encouraging such traffic and the moral advantages of discouraging it. In Mexico, for example, 60 per cent of the tourist revenue comes from 90 million US citizens driving over the border and spending $900 million in the red-light districts of Tijuana, Ciudad Juarez, Nuevo Laredo and Matamoros. These 'Boys towns' as the Americans call them, or 'zones of tolerance' as the Mexicans euphemistically describe them, pose the dilemma outlined above to the Mexican administration. The areas are visually unattractive and act as a magnet for crime and prostitution. Were it not for the foreign exchange they generate, they would unquestionably have been closed years ago; perhaps the closing down of the 'instant divorce' business in Mexico is a sign that the 'zones of tolerance' will not be tolerated much longer. In other countries, tourists are suspected of smuggling in drugs; gentlemen with long hair are not allowed to enter Thailand or Singapore as the administrations there believe this will stamp out drug traffic. Although this last instance should not be taken too seriously, the Mexican example shows how tourism can displease those local inhabitants who do not directly benefit from tourist activities.

More seriously perhaps it demonstrates the tendency of tourist areas to go downhill. This danger is emphasized by the Overseas Development Administration.[17] 'Very few tourist centres, having declined in status, have then regained it. Usually it is a one way process involving the deterioration of facilities, misuse of resources and the spoliation of the very assets that brought the tourists in the first place.'

A further aspect of tourism which can offend local inhabitants is the second home boom. The threat here has been well summarized by New Society.

Given that the second home boom is inevitable, it must be incorporated into the rural scene on terms acceptable to the best interests of the country dwellers. If matters are left as they are – to the interplay of market forces – rural areas will have a settlement imposed on them, dictated solely by wealthy urban interests.[18]

By appropriate locational policies and a positive strategic plan relating tourist needs to general town planning objectives, the interest of residents and a *finite* number of tourists can be resolved. In the absence of such a strategic plan and with an open-ended commitment to absorb tourists, sponsored nationally, there is bound to be a conflict. As with so many of the disadvantages of tourism, the level of acceptability so far as local residents are concerned cannot be accurately described or defined in advance; it is however much easier to recognize it when it has been exceeded.

To be fair to the tourist, one must also examine the contrary hypothesis; namely that, were it not for him, the resident would be deprived of a wide range of services or would have to pay much more for others. It is said, for example, that since 20 per cent of the attendance at London Zoo is accounted for by overseas visitors, the price of entry is 20 per cent less for the resident than it would otherwise be. Many London theatres sell 80 per cent of their tickets in August to overseas visitors, making a valuable contribution to overheads in what would otherwise be a very quiet period. On the other hand, it has been argued[19] that it is *winter* demand which determines the number of theatre seats available in London as theatres require high occupancy levels in all seasons. While it is therefore doubtful whether the tourist actually creates new services which the resident would otherwise lack, in some cases his custom may keep prices down by increasing occupancy rates. However, many of the services patronized by the tourist are fully subscribed anyway – like the Proms – and the fact that the tourist accounts for a high percentage of sales does not necessarily mean that he is doing the resident community a service.

These four danger areas where saturation levels may be exceeded need constant monitoring, and regional authorities need to develop methods of seeing that they are not exceeded as a result of excessive promotion at the national level. One obvious solution is to influence national tourist policy so that the flow to each particular region is optimal – neither too high nor too low – and to convince the policy-makers that beyond a certain level further increases are counter-productive at the regional level. This remedy presupposes the existence of powerful units of regional government with appropriate research facilities and powers; and while the trend may well be for national governments to lose powers on the one hand to supra-national organizations – UN, NATO, EEC, and, on the other hand, to local government, this process does not seem to be sufficiently advanced to save some of the more vulnerable European regions. For a few, such as the south coast of Spain, it is clearly too late already.

A second solution is available through the use of planning control, which is usually the prerogative of local government. If a strategic decision can be taken as to the maximum number of tourists that an area can accommodate, that number can be converted very approximately into a corresponding number of accommodation units. Planning applications can then be dealt with in the light of that optimum figure. While this is an adequate solution in theory, in practice there are very real difficulties. Firstly, the methodology for converting tourist numbers into an equivalent number of beds – if indeed an optimal number of tourists can itself be derived – is not perfect, and it excludes mobile tourists and tourists staying with friends and relatives. Secondly, national government is usually able to reverse planning decisions on appeal. Thirdly, planning legislation and enforcement procedures are usually inadequate to cope with illegal conversion of properties from flats for residents to rooms for tourists. Planning control is therefore not yet an ideal solution, though progress is being made, belatedly, to improve its application in this respect.[20]

A third solution is for local government to place a tax on hotels and tourist accommodation. This weapon can, in theory, be used to increase the price of accommodation to balance demand with supply. More important perhaps, it can also be used to equalize the financial burden of urban renewal which, due to outmoded methods of local government finance, falls disproportionately on ratepayers. Hotel taxes are now common in Europe and there is pressure for their introduction in the UK.[21] As they could solve two problems at once, they are worth further examination in the UK context.

It has been argued that it is the local community which bears the cost of providing the tourist infrastructure, and that the pattern of ownership of the tourist industry is now such that the local community no longer receives the benefits to which it is entitled. If the money spent by the tourist immediately leaves the area it cannot then generate further wealth in that community, nor increase the velocity of money circulating in that area. In the interests of the locality, the money should stay in that locality and change hands often within it. Each transaction triggered off in the area will then add to the incomes and wealth of those living there – assuming that they dispose of their goods and services at a profit. But hotels are no longer owned by individuals living in the area; they do not buy their goods from those trading in the area; in fact the tourist's pound disappears from an area very quickly.

The new hotels in London are being built by international hotel companies, international airlines and travel conglomerates. This is a phenomenon common to the whole of Europe; a study of hotel ownership in the Italian Alps[22] showed that local ownership was only predominant in the lower valleys – the traditional summer resort areas – and the newer developments, higher up the mountains, were financed by outside interests. This trend in the tourist industry means that the tourist money is siphoned off at an early stage to a central pool, where it is then expended making central purchases from areas outside the tourist destination. As with the distributive trades, the 'multiples' are increasing their share of the market and the areas which benefit from this are the areas where the goods are produced, not where they are sold. The trend towards a cashless society, towards more inclusive tours and towards more international companies is accelerating this.

The traditional counter-argument is that, in spite of these trends, tourists pay rates through the hotels and that the sheer volume of expenditure must, of necessity, help oil the wheels of local commerce even if the money ultimately ends up somewhere else. More research is undoubtedly necessary to establish whether tourists contribute enough to pay for their infrastructure; but some of the available work, admittedly on a small sample of the tourist industry, shows just how easy it is to overestimate the value of the tourists' contribution in relation to their costs. For instance, on car parking provision for tourists 'the cost of provision of each (car space) is estimated at £125 per ratepayer. Such expenditure, on only one type of public facility provision, is not recovered through visitor spending.'[23] The *Financial Times* has also drawn attention to these risks.[24] 'A large proportion of those who come [to south-west England] are the 'self-cookers', the caravan holidaymakers who spend little locally having stocked up with food before leaving. It has been estimated that some councils spend more in accommodating these people through such things as car and caravan parks than they receive in holiday money generated.' Of the tourist in Tasmania it is said that he arrives with a clean shirt and a $A10 note and does not change either of them. In Hawaii, an attempt was made in 1968[25] to calculate the cost per day of public services directly attributable to the tourist. The results are reproduced below.

Function	$
Highways	·189
Airports	·249
Police protection	·058
Fire protection	·032
Sewerage	·049
Local parks, recreation etc.	·111
Total variable cost per visitor day	·688

It is a sad commentary on the way we conduct our affairs that so few destinations have carried out this exercise before developing their tourist industries. Without this information, the benefit side of the equation is included, but the cost side is not; small wonder that the answer is that tourism should be developed as fast as possible.

A tax on tourists can be the means for ensuring that a tourist area does benefit from the tourist flows it attracts and supports. The revenue from this tax can come from national government in the form of a contribution to the rate fund, central government having collected the money by taxing the tourist on entry. Such a tax, levied in the same way as an airport tax would clearly be simple and fair as it would apply to all visitors and not just those who stayed in registered accommodation. However, it could not easily take into account the differential lengths of stay, and those staying for a short time would pay the same amount as those staying for three months. Further, a complicated system of exemption would be needed at the point of payment to prevent residents returning home from paying the tax. Finally, central government might be tempted to treat the tax as just another source of revenue, with no obligation to hand it over to local authorities.

An alternative is a tax on tourist accommodation collected directly by local authorities. The justification for it is simple; on the one hand, the population in the major tourist cities is declining each year; partly through slum-clearance in the high density areas; partly through policies to decentralize employment and partly due to a voluntary movement towards more acceptable living conditions at lower densities. Yet the costs of keeping the cities going and of improving the quality of life in them are ever increasing. Where such costs are borne by the residents of the cities, as they usually are through the local rate, it means that per capita rates will rise steadily, both because urban renewal is expensive and subject to inflationary pressure, but also because there are fewer households to bear those costs. As per capita rates rise, so this will encourage even more people to leave, leaving behind fewer people to bear the ever-increasing burden, further aggravating their financial problems and accelerating the exodus. On the other hand, as the resident population is declining, so the transient population is on the increase. It is therefore equitable to look to the transient population for funds as it is increasingly the beneficiary of urban renewal. Tourists and visitors should contribute to the costs of the services which are being maintained and improved, and which are either free or loss-making; public transport, parks and open spaces, water, roads, the police force, libraries, cultural activities etc. A hotel tax is clearly a step in the right direction though it is not a final solution as many visitors do not stay in commercial accommodation. A final solution which would satisfy the most demanding welfare economist is not yet practicable, involving as it would a complicated combination of road-pricing, metering for water, sales tax, economic prices for entry to parks etc., against which there are strong social objections. A hotel tax is however a shift in the right direction in transferring the burden of costs to those who benefit and in removing indiscriminate subsidies to visitors from residents. It is also progressive in that it is paid by the richer visitor, who can afford to stay in relatively expensive commercial accommodation, while the less well-off visitor is exempted; in this respect, a hotel tax is fairer than the domestic rate which is in no way related to ability to pay.

It is generally agreed that a hotel tax would have to be high to act as a serious deterrent, and it is not usually put forward to control or ration overall demand. The Green Paper on Hotels and Tourism in London makes the point well.[26] 'Would a hotel tax deter visitors? It seems unlikely, since despite rapidly rising hotel prices over the last decade tourists have continued to flock into London in increasing numbers. Bed prices have increased at a rate of at least 50p per annum, and the cost of meals even more steeply, with no sign of any slackening in demand.' This view was reinforced by the South East Economic Planning Council, in giving its views on the Green Paper. 'To have a deterrent effect, a tax would have to be set very high indeed.'

In theory, one can raise the tax up to the level where demand equalled supply. Unless planning controls were strict, this could lead to a 'black-market' in unregistered accommodation and would tend to ration tourists on their ability to pay. This would lead to an unbalanced intake of tourists, which could be resisted on social grounds. A hotel tax therefore has some limitations as an instrument for controlling overall demand. It should be seen more as a source of additional revenue, and as a means of influencing the location, pace and nature of new hotel development.

There are many possible variations in methods of collecting a hotel tax. Firstly, one can have a flat-rate tax of a given amount per night, which is payable by every visitor staying in registered accommodation. This effectively amounts to a temporary tax on residence, and the rate can be related to the approximate costs of residence. Such a tax is relatively simple to administer and collect. Its amount would also yield direct information on the number of visitor nights being spent in any locality – always a useful statistic. A tax of this nature operates in Austria and Switzerland, and tends not to be very large. In Austria it varies from 1½–8p per night, and in Switzerland from 4½–18p per night.

While simple, this type of tax tends to be regressive. It constitutes a small percentage of the cost of staying in expensive accommodation, and a larger percentage of the cost of staying in cheaper accommodation. This disadvantage can be overcome by the second variation. This is a tax which is a fixed percentage of the accommodation part of a hotel bill. This is fairer as it is more closely related to the ability of the visitor to pay – though not necessarily to the costs he imposes on the community. While it might be administratively simpler for the hotel to tax the entire bill, rather than the accommodation section, this would be tantamount to a tax on services provided in hotels – such as hairdressing, car-hire, purchase of theatre tickets – without taxing the same services provided elsewhere. A refinement of the above is to divide registered accommodation into a number of grades, and to have a fixed tax per night for each grade. Some grades could thus be exempt and others could be taxed at £1 per night.

By varying the rates, development of certain types of accommodation can be encouraged, and this tax can be used strategically.

Finally, if the hotel tax is to be used as an instrument of strategic planning and only secondarily as a source of revenue, then the tax can be varied according to the location of the hotel. It can thus provide a financial incentive to the developer to move out from the centre of a city to the outskirts.

There is some disagreement as to the significance of a hotel tax as far as local government revenue is concerned. In London, a tax of 50p per night could provide the GLC with a revenue of £35 million towards total expenditure of £450 million. This is a small, but worthwhile contribution. But as important as the amount is the principle. A hotel tax is the instrument for the more equitable distribution of the costs of keeping cities going; an instrument which will become more important as the population drift from the cities continues and their local tax base contracts. Further, a hotel tax has a role to play in a strategic plan to ensure that hotels of the right quality are built in the right locations. How does the tourist react to being taxed either locally or nationally? Initially, there must be a feeling of resentment since he will receive no remission of his domestic taxes and may regard a tourist tax as an unwelcome additional burden. On reflection, however, he may see the equity of the arrangement. Indeed, many tourists will benefit if their own local authorities collect revenue from tourists in their turn. If part of the revenue from a tourist tax is seen to be devoted, as it should be, to the conservation of tourist areas, improvement of tourist amenities and information services, it will surely be appreciated.

To conclude, there are therefore dangers that some of the more popular tourist destinations will be saturated by tourists; this can happen through excessive national promotion campaigns which ignore the impact on the regions, or through inadequate understanding of the complex relationships between the growth of tourism and urban economics; or through inadequate machinery to enforce optimal tourist policies. While some solutions are visible, none are yet sufficiently developed.

Numerous examples of these dangers have already been given; a final one concerns the Swiss Alps.

In the Alps, the short-term local advantages accrued through tourism have been increases in land prices, seasonal winter employment and the development of small guest-houses. But in the long run, higher land prices destroy local agriculture, seasonal employment is created for non-local people and large hotels readily displace the family pension. In terms of industrial, economic activity such transformations of the rural environment are common enough. Tourism, however, is no less an industry than steel manufacture and its introduction into Alpine alleys has been no less destructive of total population patterns and raditional culture than if each hotel had been a blast furnace.[27]

Over the next decade, conflicts of interest between tourist egions and national government are likely to be more frequent .nd more serious. For this reason, urgent attention should be paid o the development of machinery to avoid these conflicts and to ormulate a national tourist policy which contributes towards the .chievement of regional objectives instead of threatening to des- roy them.

7 Tourism and National Government

The attitude of national government towards tourism differs in several major respects from that of local or regional government which was examined in the previous chapter. This difference in approach can be traced back to the responsibilities of national government which differ both in degree and in kind from those of local government. In particular, the former is responsible for seeing that there is an adequate supply of foreign exchange to purchase essential imports; for ensuring that the level of economic activity is such that there is no widespread and persistent unemployment; for maintaining a rate of economic growth which is not embarrassingly less than that achieved by its neighbours; and for projecting a favourable 'public image' of that country abroad. These responsibilities are clearly more onerous than the relatively limited and humdrum duties of local government; and they frequently require a different approach to tourism.

It is a safe prediction that this approach of national government with its encouragement of an ever-expanding tourist industry, will lead increasingly to conflict with local or regional government which often views the development of the tourist industry as a threat to the environment and as an obstacle to the achievement of other more important objectives. The reasons for regional government holding this view were analysed in the previous chapter, and indeed this conflict is already visible where, for example, national government proposes new airports for the tourist industry in parts of the country where local residents would rather be left in peace. The possible development of V-TOL and S-TOL aircraft, with their requirement for landing places near city centres, may well bring this conflict into the towns as well.

There are of course powerful arguments why a country should promote its tourist industry, and conflict of the type outlined is no always inevitable. The arguments for promoting tourism have been developed and refined by tourist authorities and Ministries of Tourism, and publicized with all the resources at their disposal. They are set out at the beginning of this chapter, and then the other side of the argument – usually ignored by the tourist authorities – is examined.

Firstly, tourism is a source of foreign exchange. No country has ever admitted that its reserves of gold and foreign exchange are more than adequate, and few have escaped balance of payments' crises in the past decade. Any industry, therefore, which generates foreign exchange is likely to receive fiscal incentives and moral support from the government, probably at the expense of other industries which have a high import content or which do not export. Further, the foreign exchange earned by tourism is earned more conveniently than that from manufactured goods. There is no problem of packaging the product at a factory, transporting it to the docks, shipping it overseas and patiently awaiting payment. The customer brings himself to the point of sale, at his own expense, and takes immediate delivery of the services.

The importance of tourism as a source of foreign exchange is shown by Figure 3. Spain derives over one third of her foreign exchange from tourism, a dependence on one industry probably unparalleled in Western Europe. Spain's nearest rival in this respect is Guernsey, where tourism has overtaken the flower industry and is fast approaching the tomato industry. 25 per cent of Guernsey's foreign exchange comes from tourism, and the percentage for Jersey may well be higher.

The foreign exchange motive is particularly noticeable in Eastern European countries, where it is difficult to earn 'hard' currencies. A painstaking analysis by Soviet statisticians has revealed that the average profit, if that be the right word, from one tourist is equal to the export of nine tons of coal, fifteen tons of oil, or two tons of grain. Further, if Lake Baikal were exploited as a tourist centre, it would earn twice as much hard currency as the total export of oil from USSR – without depleting its stock of raw materials.

Secondly, tourism is a growth industry – and growing faster than most other export industries. Any government which is

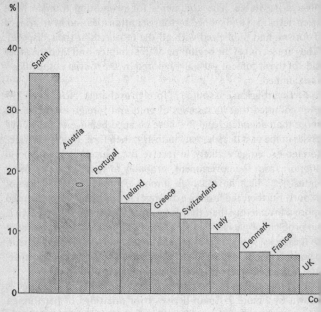

Figure 3.
Receipts from international tourism as a percentage of total export earnings. (source: *Tourism in OECD Member Countries 1970*, OECD, Paris, 1971, p. 280)

minded to assist its export industries would be well advised to select those industries whose products are going to be increasingly in demand. As was shown in Chapter 3, as personal incomes rise, so a higher percentage of that income is spent on holidays and travel. In the words of the economist, demand for tourism is elastic. Faced with the choice of assisting exports of food, clothing, motor-vehicles or tourism, a government would be well advised to choose tourism, as expenditure on tourism is going to increase faster than expenditure on the other commodities.

Thirdly, tourism may be an industry where a country has an inbuilt competitive advantage over other countries, or even, as with some types of tourism, a complete monopoly. A country which is endowed with reserves of oil, gold or diamonds would naturally concentrate its industrial and export activity on these industries. It would be a mistake to ignore such valuable raw materials and to concentrate on other industries where it lacked this competitive advantage. Although conventional economic theory has not yet extended this argument to tourist attractions, it is of course equally applicable. Historic monuments, pleasant scenery, good beaches, sun or snow are as valuable to a country as more tangible resources such as oilwells and goldmines; perhaps they are even more valuable as they are less exhaustible. Countries with a competitive advantage as far as such tourist resources are concerned should exploit them for exactly the same reasons as they should exploit any other natural resource. While most are now doing so, one or two are not. It has been said of Antigua, for example, that it has all the ingredients of a successful tourist industry apart from tourists.

Fourthly, development of the tourist industry may promote a better image of that country in the eyes of the world and thereby enable it to achieve other objectives. Eastern European countries see tourism to their countries as a means of breaking down seemingly unjustified prejudice against their way of life. The right-wing régimes in Spain and Greece would probably have received harsher treatment from more liberal European governments were they not such popular tourist destinations. Rhodesia would have been hard-pressed for economic survival in the months following UDI had it not been for the valuable foreign exchange which its tourist industry earned – £11·5 million in 1969, 80 per cent of which came from South Africans.

Fifthly, turning to internal considerations, tourism is a source of employment. Tourism is a highly labour-intensive industry which can offer employment to the semi-skilled and unskilled. In countries, or areas, where there is high unemployment, tourism can provide moderately quick relief. Even in areas with low unemployment, it can raise activity rates by generating employment for those who would otherwise not work at all, such as the retired, or married women seeking part-time employment. Tourism can thus promote national prosperity as well as international liquidity.

Finally, related to the above, tourism can be the instrument of a regional policy aimed at achieving an equitable balance between

Country	Loans				Guarantee of loans				Subsidies				Fiscal incentives		
	1966	1967	1968	1969	1966	1967	1968	1969	1966	1967	1968	1969	1966	1967	1968
Austria	x	x	x	–	–	–	–	x	1)	1)	1)	x1)	x	x	x
Belgium	x	x	x	x	x	x	x	x	1)	1)	1)	1)	x	x	x
Canada	–	–	–	–	x	x	x	x	–	–	–	–	–	–	–
Denmark	–	–	–	–	–	–	–	–	–	–	–	–	–	–	–
Finland	..	..	..	..	–	x	x	x	1)	1)	1)	1)	–	–	–
France	x	x	x	x	..	–	–	–	1)	1)	1)	1)	x	x	x
Germany	x	x	x	x	x	x	x	x	1)	1)	1)		–	–	–
Greece	..	x	x	x	..	..	..	..	..	..	..	..	..	x	x
Iceland	x	x	x	x	–	–	–	–	–	–	–	–	–	–	–
Ireland	–	–	–	–	x	x	x	x	x1)	x1)	x1)	1)	x	x	x
Italy	–	–	–	x	–	–	–	–	–	1)	1)	x1)	–	–	–
Japan	x	x	x	x	–	–	–	–	–	–	–	–	x	x	x
Luxembourg	–	x	x	x	–	x	x	x	1)	1)	1)	1)	–	–	–
Netherlands	x	x	x	x	x	x	x	x	1)	1)	1)	1)	..	..	..
Norway	x	x	x	x	x	x	x	x	–	–	–	–	–	–	–
Portugal	x	x	x	x	x	x	x	x	x	x	x	x	x	x	x
Spain	x	x	x	x	..	..	..	..	–	–	–	–	–	–	–
Sweden	x	x	x	x	x	x	x	x	x	x	x	x	–	–	–
Switzerland	x	x	x	x	x	x	x	x	–	–	–	–	–	–	–
Turkey	..	x	x	x	–	–	–	–	–	–	–	–	x	x	x
United Kingdom	x	x	x	x	–	–	–	–	x	x	x	x	x	x	x.
United States	–	–	–	–	–	–	–	–	–	–	–	–	–	–	–
Yugoslavia	x	x	x	x	..	..	..	..	x1)	x1)	x1)		..	x	x

Source: Information supplied by Member countries and Yugoslavia in reply to the annual questionnaire of the Tourism Committee.
(x) = existing (–) = non existing (..) = no information available
(1) = a subsidy to help cover interest charges is granted.

Figure 4.
Government aid to the tourist industry 1966-9.
Source: *Tourism in OECD Member Countries 1970*, OECD, Paris 1971, p. 142.

major industrial areas and the rest of a country. Many areas are simply not suited to industrial development – for example in the Irish Republic – and are in danger of being by-passed by an industrial society; tourism enables the wealth earned in one part of the country to be transferred in part to another. Viewed from the position of world government, the argument is equally valid. It is a method of transferring wealth from the richer countries to the poorer ones and securing a more equitable distribution of resources – nearly half the West German trade surplus in 1971 was extinguished by the deficit on foreign travel.

In deference to the above arguments, the tourist industry throughout the world is heavily subsidized by national governments. Figure 4 shows which OECD countries give which type of financial assistance; it is published by the OECD tourist committee and needs to be interpreted with care. For example, the final column shows that in 1969 both Austria and the United Kingdom gave fiscal incentives to their tourist industries. As far as Austria was concerned, the incentive was the very valuable one of 80 per cent exemption from turnover tax for the whole of the accommodation industry. As far as the UK was concerned, the 'incentive' was the entitlement to a refund of Selective Employment Tax by a very small number of hotels in certain rural parts of development areas. Other incentives vary from country to country; in Yugoslavia, the salaries paid to hotel staff are exempt from federal income tax. In Portugal, hotels are exempt from property and industrial tax for ten years. In Japan, travel agents are exempt from income tax on revenue earned by selling inclusive tours to Japan to foreigners. Because government incentives to tourism are changing so fast, it is difficult to say which country gives its tourist industry the most favourable treatment; it must however be difficult to imagine more favourable proposals than the investment incentives granted to foreign hotel developers by the Tunisian Government. There is a five-year exemption from corporation tax on profits, with the right to carry forward any loss to subsequent years. (How a loss could ever be incurred with the benefit of the following assistance is not explained.) There is an exemption from rates; access roads are constructed at the government's expense and the public utilities are brought to the site free of charge. The government acts as guarantor of any bank loan to build the hotel, up to half its total cost; and most of the balance can be borrowed from semi-governmental institutions at favourable interest rates. The developer can repatriate his capital and his profits whenever he wishes, and the government guarantees not to increase any taxes for twenty-five years. The convertibility of the currency is underwritten by the government, which also promises not to nationalize or confiscate the hotel. Short of the Minister of Tourism personally undertaking to change the sheets, it is difficult to imagine more favourable treatment.

While these proposals may be exceptional, the tourist industries in most countries are in receipt of substantial government funds. In addition to the assistance mentioned above, there are the subsidies dealt with in a previous chapter to airlines and airports, and the promotional budgets of tourist authorities. Because of the competition between countries to expand tourism, there is an alarming tendency to match the degrees of assistance given by the most generous governments, lest any price advantage be lost.

Economic logic has been left far behind, and the Gilbertian situation is being approached whereby it will pay everyone to be a tourist because of the subsidies to which he is entitled; and it will pay no one to be a resident because of the high levels of taxation needed to subsidize the tourist industry. Already it is cheaper for one of our old age pensioners to spend the winter months of 1972–3 in the Mediterranean at £5·65 per week inclusive through Sun Air Holidays than to stay in his own home. In the words of a company spokesman 'the basic costs of the least expensive holidays can easily be covered by the old age pension, and, according to published figures, it is far less expensive to send people abroad than to maintain them in local authority homes.'[1]

Financial assistance has been justified on the basis of the six reasons put forward earlier. There are three main arguments against such assistance; one, which will be expanded later on in this chapter, is that the disadvantages of a growing tourist industry can outweigh the advantages; the second is that it is regressive. It is worth pointing out that these large sums of money to assist the tourist industry are not only given at the expense of other industries, but that they come out of the resident taxpayer's pocket. They therefore constitute a subsidy from the resident taxpayer to the visiting tourist, whose costs of visiting are reduced by the amount of the subsidy. This is a manifestly inequitable transaction since the visiting tourist tends to have an above-average income already – as was shown in Chapter 3 – and the residents of the principal tourist receiving countries tend to have below average incomes. Assistance to the tourist industry is therefore a regressive tax, being particularly unfair on the residents of countries like Spain and Italy, whose governments assist the tourist industry considerably, and particularly favourable to residents of countries like the US, whose governments do not assist the tourist industry to the same extent and who are the most frequent travellers overseas. The third reason for not giving financial assistance is that it is not the most important or effective means of encouraging the tourist industry anyway. This point is well made by the Foreign and Commonwealth Office in a booklet for the benefit of its economic planning staff responsible for promoting tourism in developing countries.

In general, investment incentives would appear to be of only marginal influence in attracting development companies. . . since a considerable part of the overall pecuniary benefit of tourism comes from tax takings, it is important that they should not be diminished by overgenerous or unnecessary tax holidays. From discussions with various people involved in tourism, it would appear that investment incentives are much less important in attracting investment than are say (a) a positive attitude by the recipient government to tourism development (b) absence of red tape (c) governmental provision of adequate infrastructure.[2]

Experience in the UK would support this. Under the Hotel Development Incentive scheme, which expired in March 1971, some £51 million is payable by the English Tourist Board to hotel developers.[3] Nearly half of it is going to hotel developers in London, who would have built most of those hotels anyway. In London, the major constraint has never been finance, but planning permission. Hotels in London have been securing a median rate of return on funds invested of around 17 per cent,[4] and at this level there is no need for additional financial incentives. The impact of the scheme was simply to bring forward proposals already in the pipelines so that they could qualify for a grant; it is most unlikely that it caused any hotel to be built that would not otherwise have been built, and to that extent it constituted a waste of public money.

A more fundamental question than whether or not financial assistance is the correct method of helping the tourist industry is whether or not the tourist industry should be helped by national government at all. It is a question which is rarely asked and which is seldom answered. But in order to balance the formidable list of advantages conventionally adduced to the tourist industry, it is necessary to examine those countries where tourism has, for one reason or another, caused very serious problems and to put these on the other side of the balance sheet. Only then is it possible to make an impartial assessment about the treatment which the industry should receive from national government.

The disadvantages which have already arisen from the growth of tourism can be divided into four main headings; social, economic, environmental and – for want of a better expression – administrative.

The social problems which have often accompanied the growth of tourism are numerous, but the principal ones are as follows; social friction arising from the importation of foreign workers and their families to man the lower-paid jobs in the industry; the 'confrontation' effect which can result from the better-off traveller giving orders to the less well-off native; the resentment of residents having to share 'their' services with others; the effect on densities of living in the tourist cities; and the disappearance of local cultures and customs in the face of tourist development.

These social problems are most clearly visible in the Caribbean Islands where tourist development has often been rapid and unplanned. There, resentment of the tourist has grown so much that guards with guns patrol hotel grounds in Jamaica, and, in Puerto Rico *Indipendentistas* bomb American-owned hotels. The *Financial Times* may have overstated the case; 'The supporters of tourism as the main industry for the Caribbean seem blind to the fact that in Cuba a decade ago and in Jamaica at present tourism was and is responsible for social frictions with completely unforeseen consequences.'[5] But their criticism is on the right lines.

Nearer home, there are clear social problems in Spain arising from the growth of tourism. Allegations have been made recently that tourists are responsible for a new wave of colonialism. In November 1971, the Madrid newspaper *A B C* accused the twenty-five million tourists who visit Spain each year of turning large parts of the country into an 'alien land where foreign languages are spoken, foreign currency is accepted and Spaniards discriminated against. In a thousand and one small and big things, we detect the existence of a new colonialism – tourism – being imposed on us in a way which is plainly dangerous.' In April 1972, a letter in the same newspaper complained that it was easy to book a hotel in Ibiza if one spoke English and did it through a travel agency in London, but very difficult if one was a Spaniard and tried to do it in Spain.

The same sort of resentment is visible in Russia, where there are night clubs where only tourists are admitted, and in Romania, where special shops exist where only tourists can buy goods at very favourable rates of exchange.

At the root of this particular aspect of the problem, whatever the country, is the feeling of residents that 'other people are taking over our country'. It is an attack of xenophobia which is very understandable and it could well develop into an infectious epidemic if tourist authorities continue to ignore the symptoms.

In colonial countries, this resentment takes a slightly different form which is well described by the Foreign and Commonwealth Office.[6] 'The problem of social unrest caused by tourism is very much linked to both the colonial and racial hang-up as, having achieved political freedom and independence, the people now find themselves having to wait on the white man, now in the guise of the tourist.' While resentment is generally focused on the tourist, it sometimes rebounds; in the Caribbean, the hotel proprietors are often white and rich, and the porters and waiters are black and poor. In those cases, the tourist industry highlights racial disparities and creates internal resentments. Again, in Greece, the government has allocated £1 million to help owners of large private houses finance the adaptation of those houses so that they can be rented to better-off tourists in the peak months. This, understandably, has caused resentment for those Greeks who live in squalid housing conditions and maintain that they should have had first call on any funds available. Again the tourist industry can therefore be the unwitting instrument for fanning social unrest.

Behind the hostility towards tourists is the broad question of national identity, about which so little is known. It is however clear that if the trend towards dilution continues, a point would be reached where tourist destinations would have as much national character as a busy international airport. The Spanish Government's Tourist Development Plan, envisaging 49·5 million tourists in 1980 compared with a resident population of 35 million must have social repercussions, though as yet little may be known about their extent. A good place to establish what those repercussions might be is the Dutch half of the Island of St Martin; a resident population of 7,000 plays host to 130,000 visitors a year – all in 16 square miles. This ratio of 18 to 1 is twice as high as that in Bermuda, and if one maintains that the objective of a tourist plan should be to absorb without altering, then it is clear that these ratios can only be too high.

In addition to this dilution effect, incoming tourists increase the densities at which people live and this has social repercussions. It is one of the more confusing paradoxes of today's society that those countries which are most concerned about the harmful effects of a rising population are exactly those which are busily adding to their own *de facto* population most by encouraging inward tourism. For example, overseas visitors to the UK spent 100 million nights there in 1971. This is numerically equivalent to an addition of 270,000 people to the permanent resident population; and almost the same as the natural increase in the population that year. It would appear to be, at worst, wholly inconsistent and, at best, slightly unpatriotic to exhort the resident population to control its numbers in the interest of reducing densities and, at the same time, to urge those who live overseas to visit our crowded island. The UK is already the fifth most densely populated country in the world, and, if England is looked at on its own, no country is more densely populated.

Population density, mid 1969[7]

Country	Inhabitants per sq. mile
England	917
Netherlands	914
Belgium	818
Japan	715
W. Germany	635
(United Kingdom)	591
Italy	466
France	236
USA	57
Sweden	47

In Bermuda densities of 53,000 resident Bermudians are 2,400 per square mile; in the peak tourist season this rises nearly 50 per cent to 3,300.

In addition to importing tourists, an expanding tourist industry often needs to import foreign workers to take up the new posts. This can give rise to social problems, particularly where the foreign workers so imported are of a different race, colour, or creed to the native population. In Bermuda, the government curbed the expansion of the tourist industry because the immigrants needed to staff it were becoming an active and embarrassing political force. In Western Europe, the social problems which have resulted from immigration – particularly coloured immigration – are not in dispute. It would however be fairer to blame a lack of mutal understanding and sheer prejudice for these problems, rather than the employer of the labour. However, in the U K, one seventh of the work-force in hotel and catering are foreign, and that percentage is increasing. It is only sensible to moderate that increase to the capacity of society to absorb immigrants, whatever one's view about the economic benefits of tourism or the futility of racial prejudice.

This dependence of the tourist industry on foreign labour is causing particular problems in Switzerland. Swiss hoteliers say they need 50,000 foreign workers to staff their hotels, yet the quota for all Swiss industry is only 21,000. If all the 50,000 were admitted, over a third of all those employed in the tourist industry – 140,000 – would be foreign; further, the problems of accommodating them and their families would be enormous.

If the jobs which the tourist industry generated were ones with good pay and good working conditions, then the edge would be taken off these social problems. But they are not – particularly in hotel and catering. A survey by the Hotel and Catering Industry Training Board showed that conditions of work and prospects were poor and this inevitably has social repercussions. Two thirds of the work-force have to work on Saturdays or Sundays, and the hours of work are often such as to disrupt normal family life. The environment in which many of them work is far from satisfactory and the survey showed that career prospects were poor; some 64 per cent of the experienced staff surveyed had never progressed beyond the level of operative, and 72 per cent had not improved their status at all since they first entered the industry. The National Hotels Syndicate in Spain has complained that 'thousands of hotel workers are finding themselves at nearly minimum salary' because of the 'financial crisis faced by the hoteliers forced to concede very low prices to foreign tourist groups'.[8] The effect of stimulating the tourist industry can therefore increase the number of less attractive jobs whereas a government should try to influence events so that the numbers of these jobs decrease.

The disruptive effect of tourism on local cultures is one of the saddest effects of the industry, threatening to result in a monotonous world non-culture that replaces regional differences. This threat is fortunately being recognized; at Fiji's eleventh annual tourism convention[9] the Minister of Tourism attacked 'foreign investors who have no conception of local problems and are insensitive to local feelings'. Members of that government in Fiji, fully aware that it would be wrong to rely on sugar as the basis of the economy, are openly expressing reservations about diversification into the tourist industry because of the socially disastrous changes it would impose on the Fijian way of life. Culture, after all, is about people and patterns of everyday life – not monuments and souvenirs.

Dr Frances Cottington has tried to prove a correlation between the growth of tourism and the increase in divorces in Hawaii. The growth of the tourist industry has led to increased demand for maids and waitresses to work in the new hotels, a demand which has been eagerly met by the wives of the low-paid, agricultural workers. The opportunity for infidelity provided by the tourist industry is, apparently, responsible for a doubling of the divorce rate in four years.[10]

While this instance need not be taken too literally, the social problems which can accompany a growing tourist industry are serious, and frequently ignored. Research is needed to clarify these problems, and the whole process of tourist development needs amending so that social considerations are taken into account in the decision-making process.

The economic disadvantages which can arise from an expanding tourist industry can be divided into several sub-headings; the effect on growth of having a sizeable proportion of a country's labour-force engaged in a service activity with poor productivity prospects; the inflationary consequences of excessive tourist activity; the unfavourable impact on the balance of payments (in spite of claims to the contrary); the heavy infrastructure costs which are usually a prerequisite of tourist development; and the loss of control over the economy due to the absence of fiscal regulators where taxes are low or non-existent in order to encourage foreign investment; and the overdependence of an economy on one product.

In 1961 these disadvantages were summarized by J. Renucci.[11] 'Capital investments come from sources exterior to the development projects; they aim at satisfying demands from outside the island and create profits which, for the most part, leave the island.' It is now generally admitted[12] that damage has been done to the economies of developing countries because of over-optimistic work in the early 1960s – particularly as a result of the Zinder[13] and Checchi[14] reports, which exaggerated the benefits of tourism and overestimated the multiplier effect. Though too little is still known about the effects of tourism on an economy, it is possible to put together some general propositions. If a tourist spent his money in the same way as a resident, his presence could not, *per se*, accelerate or retard growth. But tourist expenditure, by its very nature, is directed towards labour intensive service industries, rather than capital intensive manufacturing industries. Figure 5 shows the percentage of total consumers' expenditure in various countries which is accounted for by tourism and is a measure of this influence of tourist activity. Tourists can therefore shift the total direction of consumers' expenditure, and it is the direction in which this shift is made which can retard growth. The argument is essentially a simple one, maintaining that if a country's labour-force is enticed towards a service industry with a poor productivity record, below average earnings, low value added, a high staff turnover and a large element of seasonal unemployment, then economic growth may well be slower than if that labour was not so enticed. The British Tourist Authority has estimated that 25 per cent of tourists' expenditure in the UK goes on accommodation, 25 per cent on restaurants – including hotel restaurants – 28 per cent on shopping, 12·5 per cent on transport within the UK and 9·5 per cent on entertainment, travel agencies, banking services etc. These are predominantly labour-intensive industries, and £1 spent on them requires more labour than £1 spent on most other industries. Perhaps the largest employers in the tourist industry are the hotels, and a recent survey carried out by the Hotel and Catering Industrial Training Board confirms the traditional view of this industry as one with low pay, high turnover and poor prospects. A random survey of 1,880 workers in the UK hotel industry revealed the following results.

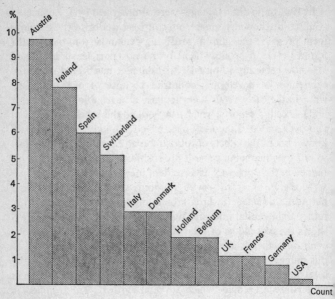

Figure 5.
Expenditure by international tourists as a percentage of total consumer expenditure in selected countries.

Unskilled kitchen operatives account for 35 per cent of the industry's labour-force, and, if one classifies waiters and barmen, together with their female counterparts, as unskilled, then 60 per cent of the industry's labour-force is unskilled. By including maids and cleaners in this category the proportion is in fact two thirds. In view of this high percentage of unskilled labour, earnings in the industry are well below average. A nationwide survey of 150 hotels carried out by the University of Strathclyde's Scottish Hotel School showed that it cost an average of less than £700 to employ a hotel worker in Britain. The average profit, or value added per employee, was only £300 before interest and tax. This is well below average as is shown by the following table.[15]

Net Output per £ of Wages and Salaries = $\dfrac{\text{Total Value Added}}{\text{Total wages} + \text{Salaries}}$

£4·16	Coal and petroleum products
£2·77	Chemicals and allied industries
£2·74	Gas, electricity and water
£2·61	Food, drink and tobacco
£1·94	Other manufacturing industries
£1·86	Bricks, pottery, glass, cement etc.
£1·84	Mining and quarrying
£1·83	Leather goods and fur
£1·81	Paper, printing and publishing
£1·81	Other metal goods
£1·80	Metal manufacture
£1·80	Electrical engineering
£1·79	Textiles
£1·78	Timber, furniture
£1·78	Mechanical engineering
£1·67	Clothing and footwear
£1·63	Instrument engineering
£1·44	Vehicles
£1·43	Hotel and catering
£1·20	Shipbuilding and marine engineering
£1·88	All manufacturing industries

For every £1 spent on wages, the coal and petroleum products industry generates £3·16 towards overheads and profit. The hotel industry generates a mere 43p, and, apart from shipbuilding and marine engineering, is the least productive industry in the table. (The fact that hotel and catering trades employ a large proportion of part-time and female labour is irrelevant as the measurement relates to output per £ of wages, not output per employee.)

Evidence is available that the tourist industry does have significant advantages over manufacturing and agricultural industry in assisting growth in the less developed countries. '$65 million investment in tourism up to 1973 will increase GDP by $53 million; an increase in capital stock rather less than the increase necessary to secure the same increase in GDP in manufacture, and about the same necessary in agriculture.'[16] What the above comment does not bring out is that investment in tourist infrastructure is of little benefit to the residents of less developed countries. They are not intensive users of hotels or airports, whereas investment in other industries could be of more tangible benefit to them.

All this is not to say that the tourist industry is undesirable because it always retards growth; some jobs are very highly paid. In 1970, pilots flying jumbo jets for United Airlines were paid $57,000 per year for 75 hours flying per month.[17] It is to say that promotion of the tourist industry at the expense of other industries, as far as employment is concerned, may conflict with other objectives – namely raising the general level of prosperity by structuring the country's employment in such a way that jobs with better pay and prospects are encouraged where possible. This potential conflict is not always made explicit with the result that tourism is sometimes promoted against a country's best interests. The right answer – if right answer there be – depends on the use to which the resources devoted to tourism would be put if they were released. Where there is high unemployment, a relatively unskilled labour-force and few alternative sources of employment – as for example in Mauritius – then stimulation of the tourist industry may well be a correct course of action. The danger appears to be at the next stage of economic development, where unemployment and under-employment have been reduced, the labour force is better educated and an infrastructure exists which might support other industries. Continuing dependence and emphasis on tourism may no longer be economically justifiable.

It is a matter of regret that inadequate work on this subject has been undertaken. 'Not only is there no agreement on the methodology to be used in the more theoretical aspects of tourism economics, there has been no work as yet done on the effect of tourism on countries either in terms of the economic effect and the stages of the growth of tourism, or in terms of the socio-psychological effect.'[18]

Fortunately, since that comment was made, some evidence has become available of the economic implications of the growth of the tourist industry in Spain. It is worth quoting in some detail as it shows how the country with what is commonly regarded as the most successful tourist industry has totally mismanaged its development.

The pattern of investment that emerges (from these figures) clearly indicates that the Development Plan was concerned essentially with

those economic activities related to tourism and its immediate requirement. Insofar as the Plan was intended to guide the development
strategy of the country as a whole, it appears that economic development was understood to mean the co-ordination of the market forces
propelled by the tourist revolution but not their conscious re-orienta-
tion. The course of action went along with the autonomous forces of
expansion rather than directing those forces to an intentional course of
development. This was, no doubt, the easiest course to take – that is, to
acquiesce in a pattern of investment which would be shaped by the
allocation of resources brought about by tourism. . . The Development
Plan therefore, was not a conscious and intentional effort to reshape
the natural course of the economy's growth. The Plan therefore did
not make the most of the opportunities afforded by the income
derived from tourism; it even appears to have intensified the problems
of the economy. The excessive concentration in infrastructure investments to the detriment of industrial growth, as well as the huge expansion of the service sector, accentuated the lop-sided character of
the economy and aggravated the sectoral tensions between agriculture
and industry.[19]

The message is essentially that the energy of the tourist industry
should be properly harnessed and put to beneficial use; instead,
in Spain the industry has galloped ahead, dragging behind it the
creaking and swaying structure of the Spanish economy.

In order to shed more light on the effect on economic growth of
a well-developed tourist industry, Figure 6 shows the relationship
between standards of living – defined as per capita incomes converted to dollars at current exchange rates – and developed
tourist industries – defined by reference to their earnings from
tourism as a percentage of all earnings of foreign exchange.

It is quite clear from the graph that the more developed a
country's tourist industry, the lower the standard of living of its
inhabitants. This argument is not conclusive, and leads naturally
to another one; if it is not the case that those countries with highly
developed tourist industries currently enjoy the highest standards
of living, are they at least narrowing the gap between themselves
and wealthier countries?

This hypothesis can be tested by relating the growth rates of
the economies of various countries with the increase in their
revenue from tourism, and seeing whether the two factors are

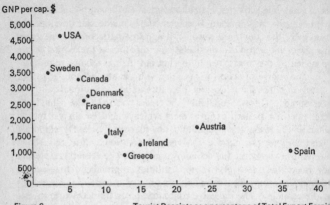

Figure 6.   Tourist Receipts as a percentage of Total Export Earni

Relationship between development of tourist industry and GNP per
capita. (source: *Tourism in OECD Member Countries 1970*, OECD,
Paris, 1971, p. 25; and national accounts of individual OECD countries.)

related. This exercise is not conclusive, which implies that there is
no clean correlation between the two factors.

The inflationary consequences[20] which tourism can cause arise
in several ways; well-off tourists can cause a general increase in
prices in shops which local residents then have to pay; a vigorous
hotel building programme can cause rises in construction costs and
therefore affect the price of homes for residents; and land prices
can increase through hotel purchase, or through purchase of
holiday homes. In the Canary Islands,[21] for example, prices have
risen 30 per cent per year for the past three years because the
Islands are a good place to retire to, or have a holiday house buil
in. In 1963, a plot of land measuring 736 square metres near San
Agustin beach changed hands for £1,512. In 1968, it was sold fo
£8,650; and in 1971 it changed hands at £27,000. Two bedroomed
bungalows in the same area cost from £12,000 to £15,000. Loca
residents, while benefiting if they sell properties, are penalized i
they are purchasing.

In Bermuda, due to the absence of a tourist plan, the rapid
expansion of tourism was unrelated to the labour supply on the
island to service it and this led to galloping wage inflation, as

employers engaged in tourist industries outbid each other for a limited pool of labour. The tourist boom pushed up the already high cost of land and houses, and added fuel to the inflationary fire. Because Bermuda is a tax-haven, the government lacked the normal fiscal and monetary weapons to deal with this problem, and was therefore forced to intervene directly to rescue the economy from the tourist boom. It has frozen new hotel development for five years to relieve some of the pressures mentioned above, and to give breathing-space to the hard-pressed building industry.[22]

The previous chapter showed how the growth of tourism locally could price out shops providing goods and services for residents and replace them with shops providing more expensive goods and services for tourists. This phenomenon means that where the former shops remain, they have to pay higher rent and rates, which are passed on to consumers through higher prices. This effectively means that domestic inflation is being induced by overseas visitors.

The unfavourable impact of tourism on the balance of payments is, on the face of it, a surprising argument put forward for criticizing growth in tourism. Yet tourism is not necessarily the great foreign exchange earner which it appears to be at first sight. Many countries have to import on a large scale to build up their tourist industries; and many more rely to a large extent on imports to keep it running. Further, due to the changing structure of the tourist industry, much tourist expenditure does not stay in the country very long. The shellfish which the Englishman eats on holiday at the Costa Brava probably came from the British Isles. Because the necessary economic analysis is all too rarely performed,[23] no one really knows how much *net* foreign exchange is retained by the tourist industry in most destination countries. However, where calculations have been made, the results are not very encouraging.

An example is Mauritius. 'Mauritius is acutely aware that the net foreign exchange benefits to the Island from inclusive tours amount only to 10 per cent of total expenditure when deductions are made from takings of overseas airlines, foreign tour operators, imports of provisions for tourists and repatriation of profits by foreign hotel developers.'[24] With such a slender margin on current account, any initial deficit on capital account – through materials being purchased for hotel building for example – might take some time to eliminate.

Other studies do not reveal such a high import content as for Mauritius; but they do suggest that it is misguided to assume that tourism has a lower import content than other industries and therefore deserves preferential treatment. In 1958, a study by Professor George Cumper of the University of West Indies showed that 39 per cent of Jamaica's tourist income went straight out of the country, the main import content being food. Further, since less than half the hotel bedrooms in Jamaica are owned by Jamaicans,[25] there is clearly a substantial leakage from that source as well. Even Israel, which probably has one of the lowest import contents of any tourist destination, loses 25 per cent through imports.[26]

Tourism has also proved a doubtful blessing to the balance of payments of the Caribbean island of St Lucia. This small island has depended for many years on its banana crop, from which it earned £2·5 million in 1969 from 85,000 tons of bananas. The tourist boom however has caused a flight of labour from the land, leaving the task of growing bananas to the landowners and their immediate families. It has been estimated that the average family unit can only manage five acres without outside help. Since many of the units are much larger, there have been disastrous effects on productivity and considerable under-utilization of land. Meanwhile, most of the food served to the tourist is imported so a large percentage of the tourist expenditure – supposedly replacing the banana as the earner of foreign currency – goes straight out of the country. The switch to tourism has strained the balance of trade and much of the profit from the hotels – which are exempt from tax – also goes abroad. The problem is of course aggravated by the peak of the tourist season coinciding with agricultural harvest and fruit picking time.

The section on the structure of the tourist industry provide part of the answer to these high import contents and leakage of foreign earnings. Increasingly the tourist industry is being dominated by international companies not based in the destina on countries. This gives rise to a related problem about the taxation of profits, and tourist authorities would be well advised to look at the history of oil refining if they wish to maximize revenue from tourism and reduce the 'leakage' referred to.

It is well-known that the oil which is drilled by the producing subsidiary of a large oil company is 'sold' at an artificially low price to the trading subsidiary of the same company, so that profit and hence tax liability in the producing country is minimized. The trading subsidiary has its headquarters in a tax-haven and it 'sells' the oil to the refining subsidiary in a developed country at a high price so that the refining subsidiary makes no profit either. Thus, by a series of complicated book-keeping exercises, the profit is generated in a country with a very low tax rate, and little or no tax is paid in the other countries.

The governments of the oil-producing countries have, understandably, responded. They have calculated more realistic or 'posted' prices for the oil drilled in their countries, rather than rely on the prices in the books of the oil companies for the computation of tax liability. The 'posted' price is multiplied by the volume of oil drilled to calculate the true profit made by the producing subsidiary.

It requires but little imagination to relate this problem of oil revenues and tax evasion to the problems of tourist revenues and tax evasion. In the future, more and more tourists will travel on inclusive tours; and the more inclusive a tourist becomes, the more he will pay to international companies owning aircraft, hotels and other tourist services. These companies can so arrange their book-keeping that the hotel subsidiaries in the destination countries make no profits and pay no tax. The trading subsidiary, located in a tax-haven, simply buys the accommodation at a cost which covers operating costs.

In the same way as the oil-producing countries have had to intervene and protect the interests of their residents, so the more developed European ones may have to do the same. The UK is guilty of extreme negligence in this respect. On its treatment of North Sea oil and gas it has been said 'revisions in UK policy are undoubtedly needed. Taxation policy on profits remains singularly ill-defined and open to abuse and there is a strong case for evolving particular oil production taxation and possibly a revision in royalty policy to ensure that oil finds bring greater direct financial benefit to the country. At the same time, there is most certainly a need to tighten up controls over changes in the composition or ownership of groups . . .'[27] If the UK is vulnerable in this respect, it is even more vulnerable with respect to its tourist industry. The most popular tourist attractions in the world are free to the tourist, who pays large sums of money to companies domiciled outside the UK for the privilege of coming to stay in London. With their experience of raw materials in mind, the African countries have seen to it that their tourist resources are not exploited in this way. Hotels are often owned by the government and in some cases tourists have to arrive on national airlines. It is perhaps ironic that while the underdeveloped countries are taking these precautions, the developed ones are not. A 'posted' price for hotels in the UK may not be far off.

Further 'leakages' take place through generous assistance to tour operators bringing in tourists; indeed Sicily gives away so much money in this respect that the net foreign exchange benefit must be almost negligible. The government gives each operator £133 for each charter flight bringing people to stay for at least a week; it adds to this a 30 per cent grant on all off-season programmes and a 10 per cent grant for main season programmes. In addition, the operator gets 13 per cent of hotel profits if his programme includes hotel accommodation. On a low-cost package holiday, the Sicilians could actually be paying for the privilege of entertaining foreign tourists.

Other drains on foreign exchange take place when expansion of the tourist industry requires the import of capital goods. In these cases an expanding tourist industry can actually be a net loser of foreign exchange even though there may be a foreign exchange surplus on current account. It is possible that Spain will meet this sort of problem if the tourist industry continues to expand fast. The Spanish Government envisages 49·5 million tourists in 1980; the Ministry of Information and Tourism, who seem to be unaware of this target, have set their sights on 45 million by 1975 and 10 million by 1980 (10 million of whom are expected to come from the UK). To meet this target, 50,000 hotel beds would have to be built each year at a cost of about £240 million. A substantial portion of this capital investment would be spent on goods and services from outside Spain and this will make considerable inroads into the net surplus on foreign exchange from tourism.

Finally, on the balance of payments implications, it is high time that a fallacy repeated time and time again by tourist authorities all over the world was exploded; tourist authorities in the better-off countries state, quite rightly, that their citizens are spending more and more money overseas and this constitutes a drain on the balance of payments. They go on to say that this 'balance of tourism' deficit must be removed by increasing the inward flow of tourists. This is equivalent to saying that because a country imports pogo-sticks it must also export pogo-sticks to avoid a deficit on the pogo-stick account; it overlooks the fact that the country may not be very good at making pogo-sticks and would earn much more foreign exchange by making hula-hoops. So with tourism; currency spent abroad by tourists can be earned in other ways than by importing tourists and it might in fact be a mistake to build up the tourist industry with this objective in mind when other industries could earn as much foreign exchange from fewer resources.

The last economic disadvantage arises when overdependence on tourism makes the economy vulnerable to changes of fashion. While tourism is indeed a growth industry and the total volume of traffic is certain to grow, in overall terms, for the foreseeable future, individual destinations may not share in that growth for a number of reasons – wars, industrial unrest or simply changes of fashion. The Irish Republic, which derives 15 per cent of its foreign exchange requirements from tourism, has been badly hit in this respect. Other countries have simply fallen out of fashion. Monaco, for example, had 70 hotels and 3,580 rooms in 1939, but 30 years later it had only 31 hotels and 1,650 rooms. The aristocracy passed it by, and the new generation of tourists could not afford it. That Monaco has learnt its lesson is shown by a statement by H R H Prince Rainier. 'It would have been neither safe nor right to put all one's eggs in one basket. The tourist trade and activity cannot alone support the principality for many obvious reasons, the first being that tourism is a changing matter and a ver fragile one at that.'[28]

The environmental disadvantages are those which all too ofte accompany the over-exploitation of tourism; despoliation of coas lines, pollution of the sea, loss of historic buildings to make wa for tourist accommodation, and loss of agricultural land for ai port development.

Perhaps the biggest environmental casualty has been th Mediterranean Sea, steadily deteriorating, largely as a result of over-development of the coast for tourist purposes. Every one of the 6,000 registered beaches in Italy is dangerously pollute according to standards decreed by the Italian Health Ministry some beaches have bacteria counts five times higher than th limit. 100,000 tons of oil are disgorged annually into the Mediter ranean together with huge quantities of untreated sewage, indus trial effluent and agricultural run-off. In July 1970, a report to th French Government warned of the disappearance of marine lif from the inshore area of the Mediterranean – marine life whic produces a large part of the oxygen which man needs to survive It pointed out that in the forty miles from Cannes to Menton ther were 195 open drains discharging untreated sewage straight into tideless sea.

As with other problems concerning tourism, the internationa machinery to deal with this particular international problem is non existent. The countries which border on the Mediterranean ar indirectly dependent on it for foreign exchange; yet instead of joining together to protect a valuable common resource, they ar accelerating an ecological breakdown by shortsighted and indis criminate development along the shores. The same is true of th River Rhine; six countries share it as an international tourist asse – Switzerland, Austria, France, Germany, Luxembourg an Holland – and, in recognition of its importance, five of them hav joined together to form the International Commission for th Protection of the Rhine against Pollution. Unfortunately thi Commission has no powers whatsoever, and, in the words of it chairman, 'Our experts from five countries do excellent work. W know what must be done to improve the situation. But I canno point to any actual measures we have taken.'[29] Meanwhile th

Rhine is gradually becoming a vast, septic sewer, stretching from the Alps to the North Sea. Just as national assets are destroyed through inadequate machinery to protect them, so international assets are similarly exposed.

Still in the Mediterranean, the building on the coasts of Southern Spain, along the Italian Riviera and the Viareggio coast and the Adriatic have destroyed completely the character of the area. Inadequate legislation and indifference by local residents are largely to blame, and while middle-class pressure groups in Spain and Italy are now agitating to put this right, they are probably too late. Hundreds of miles of coastline have been ruined irremediably by virtually uncontrolled building of hotels, restaurants, bars and houses. Beaches have been divided into unsightly allotments, and noise from juke-boxes, fumes from traffic and sheer human overpopulation pay witness to the chaos man has made of the organization of his leisure. These evil consequences are not *inherent* in the development of tourism; they just happen when tourism is developed in a thoughtless and casual way.

Some of the larger national parks in Africa are now suffering from an accumulation of overcommercialization, and this is another aspect of the environmental damage that can be caused by tourism.

Convoys of Safari cars circling round the game-viewing drives have so affected the wildlife that it is no rare sight today to come across as many as 20 or 30 vehicles laagered round a pride of lions so inured to the human environment that they make no effort to move when people and cameras emerge somewhat noisily from a ring of cars. This is not what the tourist expects to see in Africa and it is not what the authorities controlling the wildlife want either. . . The conservational aspects must not be swamped by tourism objectives. The problem facing the authorities today is the constant conflict between the priorities of tourism growth and the need to preserve wildlife sanctuaries without undue impairment to their natural state.[30]

Elsewhere in Africa the character of parks is being altered by the proximity of airports, buildings and hotels, and the sheer volume of visitors.

In London, the scale of hotel development in the more sen-

sitive parts of the capital is quite indefensible on environmenta
grounds. In particular, views of Hyde Park are dominated by ta
hotels and, in the same area, some of the newer hotels hav
replaced buildings which, whatever their shortcomings, blende
more naturally with their surroundings.

It is of course true that the development of any new industr
involves some change in the environment. The particular disad
vantage with tourism is that those changes take place where th
environment is at its most attractive and where it is most vul
nerable. Other things being equal, it would be better to develo
new industries which can take root in less sensitive locations.

The final disadvantage of tourism has been called an administra
tive one. It arises in two ways; firstly the ownership of land an
the control of components of the tourist industry are increasingl
in the hands of non-residents and of companies based elsewhere
This gives rise to serious conflicts of interest as to how the touris
industry as a whole should be developed or controlled. This prob
lem was well illustrated by the Monaco 'incident' involvin
Aristotle Onassis. The 'Société des Bains de Mer' is the backbon
of the Monegasque economy. It owns the casino, several hotels
the beach club and the sea club. Mr Onassis started to buy share
and to influence the policy of the company so that, in the eyes o
the Monegasques, quick profits were made by the company to th
detriment of Monaco as a whole. The company was therefor
nationalized, Mr Onassis' holding was acquired, and more altruis
tic policies were adopted.

The solution in Monaco was possible because resources wer
available to purchase the outside interests. In many countries th
resources are not available to finance the development of th
tourist industry, or to acquire control of it in subsequent years
The Prime Minister of Fiji, Sir Kamesis Mara, is concerned tha
profits from Fiji's tourist industry accrue to non-Fijians. Of th
eight major tour operators in Suva, for example, only one i
Fijian. A major review of government assistance to the touris
industry is now under way, and it is unlikely that foreign owner
ship of the tourist industry will continue to be encouraged.

In those cases, control and ownership rest outside the country
What has happened too often is that those outside interests hav

acquired the best sites and the beaches and have then exploited them in such a way that an overall tourist plan, devised at a later date, cannot be implemented. A good example of this is Mauritius. Development was left entirely to private industry, much of it foreign. Tourism was developed in an uncoordinated and fragmented way and, in particular, it resulted in the extravagant alienation of the best coastal sites which has now seriously prejudiced the success of any comprehensive tourist development plan. The same sort of problem has arisen in Spain, where foreign tour operators have the Spanish tourist industry and therefore the whole Spanish economy in the palm of their hands. Many of the new tourist developments in Spain are not Spanish-owned, particularly on the Costa del Sol. The Ministry of Industry has published figures showing that over £15 million is being put up by outside interests to expand the tourist facilities in that area alone.[31]

Related to this is the problem of alienation of land through tourist acquisition or through foreign settlers. In Ontario, Americans have bought land on the shores of Lake Muskoka, and locals are now denied access to that lake. In New Zealand, the government has been severely criticized by its citizens for letting Americans buy up some of the best 'high country', and the fishing and shooting rights that go with it. Some 3 per cent of Swiss real estate is now owned by foreigners and, in spite of the 'Lex van Moos' which makes land acquisition by non-residents more difficult, successful applications to buy land in 1970 were three times higher than in 1960. The problems arising from this acquisition were highlighted in 1971, when the St Gotthard Hospice was offered for sale to some Italians and Germans. There was a public outcry as this was tantamount to selling Buckingham Palace to the Americans. Fortunately the Swiss Government discovered that the St Gotthard Hospice was in a fortification zone and, as such, could not be sold to non-nationals.

Paradoxically, this issue provides one of the few examples of local government encouraging tourism in the face of opposition from central government. The Swiss cantons are usually delighted to welcome rich settlers in their areas as the loss of marginal farming land, on which they build, is a small price to pay for the benefit of high local rates and taxes. National government, taking a broader view, is concerned about the continuing 'dilution' of Swiss ownership; and this does raise a fundamental question about national identity. In the long term, what will be the difference between the countries of Europe – apart from geographical ones – if their citizens are a similar mixture of differing nationalities? The solution adopted by many countries is a ban on foreign ownership. In Mexico, for example, foreign ownership of land is forbidden within 50 kms of the coast or frontier. The Greeks have the ultimate solution; a national prayer begging for protection against invasion by the tourist!

The second administrative problem relates to the statistical confusion which arises from a more mobile population. For instance, the *Evening Standard* has proclaimed disparagingly that 'London is more drunken now than it was 100 years ago. The capital has more drunks per head of population than any other place in Britain.'[32] According to Christian Economic Social Research, who prepared a report on the subject, London's figure for 'total inebriety' was 68·8 per 10,000 population over 15 – twice as high as the next major population centre. But if some of the 'totally inebriate' were visitors to the capital and not residents, the accusations are an unwarranted libel on the peaceful and sober citizens of London. The figure of 68·8 does not apply to the resident population, but to the resident and visiting population. One might, indeed, draw the opposite conclusion, that visitors to London were unable to live up to the high standards of sobriety which Londoners have set themselves.

This example is one which need not be taken too seriously; but all too often plans for cities are made on the basis of statistics relating to the resident population and which therefore exclude the needs of the transient population. The first Greater London Traffic Survey excluded movements by visitors; open space requirements in London are on the basis of so many acres per 1,000 resident population[33] and therefore exclude the needs of visitors. Elsewhere plans for shopping requirements and public transport often exclude visitors and are therefore inadequate.

What is the answer to all these national and international problems which the development of the tourist industry, albeit unwit tingly, is creating? How can governments respond in order to diminish these problems? There are clear indications that the degree of assistance given to the tourist industry exceeds that which can be justified by rational argument. All too often, governments do not ask themselves the basic question, 'Why should we subsidize the tourist industry?' The only time the UK government appears to have addressed itself to this question is through the House of Commons Expenditure Committee which skated superficially over the subject in three minutes.[34]

There are disadvantages in developing the tourist industry which are either inadequately appreciated, ignored or suppressed; and some of the advantages ascribed to tourism have yet to be proven and in some cases may even be having the opposite effect to the one claimed. The right answer is surely to identify in advance the appropriate volume of tourism which a country can absorb, to derive from that a coherent tourist plan with predetermined objectives and to assemble the machinery to implement it. Planning for tourism must be completely integrated with planning for other objectives, and growth must be restrained where it prejudices the attainment of these other objectives. The Overseas Development Administration have put their finger on the problem:

> Almost without exception, the tendency in the tourist business is to push 'development', that is to get more tourists, and to increase expenditure per tourist. What is lacking however is programme development that will control the tourism process... the fact is that a community or country that invites millions of tourists and at the same time institutes no programme to protect itself will be overwhelmed.[35]

The main obstacle to this rational approach is, in most countries, the Ministry of Tourism. Where there is a powerful ministry responsible for promoting tourism, which is under no obligation to reconcile the consequences of its activities with other ministries, an unbalanced approach is inevitable. There is never an equally powerful voice putting forward the contrary view that tourism should be restrained. The activities of these increasingly powerful departments need analysing so that one can assess the broader implications of what they are doing, and in particular so that one can see to what extent the objectives mentioned earlier are being

achieved and to what extent unforeseen consequences are inter-
fering.

The activities of the tourist authorities vary from the broadly
laissez-faire right through the spectrum to the highly interven-
tionist and cover, in that order, the following; the provision of
information services to those tourists who have already arrived;
the promotion overseas of the country concerned as a tourist destination; the supervision of the tourist industry, for example,
through the grading of hotels, registration of travel agents or
administration of a hotel reservation scheme; and, as an extreme,
the ownership and control of all the components of the tourist
industry. An analysis of tourist promotion costs carried out by
IUOTO showed that member organizations in 67 countries
spent £38 million in 1970. In that year Europe overtook North
America as the major spender on promotion, disbursing £23 million
of which the UK accounted for £3 million. (These figures exclude
advertising by national airlines, which are usually an arm of the
government.)

The impact of this expenditure is extremely difficult to assess;
the tourist authorities maintain that a high volume of advertising
is essential if a country is to hold its share in this highly competitive market. One would hardly expect them to say otherwise,
and there is some evidence to substantiate this view. Perhaps the
most convincing is a before-and-after study commissioned by the
United States Travel Service from Arthur D. Little Inc. The terms
of reference of the study were to see how travel to the US from
various other countries had increased before the establishment of
the US Travel Service, and to relate that increase to socio-economic
characteristics of the countries concerned and to the cost of travelling to the USA. This equation was then applied to the same
socio-economic characteristics after the establishment of the US
Travel Service to see whether the propensity to visit the USA had
increased by more than was expected. In those cases where it had,
it was concluded that this was due to the marketing activities of
the USTS.

If one wanted to support the cynic who maintains that one can
prove anything with statistics, this example is an ideal one. It is
possible to prove, equally conclusively, that the influence of

marketing is negligible. Column 1 of Figure 7 shows how the number of arrivals of Swedish visitors in the UK increased between 1950 and 1966. Column 2 shows how many Swedes 'ought' to have arrived in the UK, on the basis of an equation relating the propensity of the Swedes to visit the UK to the cost of travel between the two countries and to broad social and economic characteristics of the Swedes. It can be seen at once that the equation is extremely accurate indeed, although it takes no account of advertising expenditure, which is meant to have a significant effect on arrivals.

Predictive accuracy of regression analysis of Swedish arrivals in the UK.

Year	1 Arrivals, as per Home Office	2 Arrivals as predicted by equation	3 Residual (column 1 minus column 2)
1950	20,361	19,998	363
1951	21,421	21,377	44
1952	21,638	21,607	31
1953	21,559	22,010	−451
1954	23,071	23,124	−53
1955	27,751	27,453	298
1956	25,742	26,806	−1064
1957	25,564	24,622	942
1958	25,934	26,034	−100
1959	29,499	29,773	−274
1960	32,674	32,552	122
1961	36,919	36,293	626
1962	37,547	37,102	445
1963	42,521	42,791	−270
1964	46,605	48,857	−2252
1965	57,238	55,643	1595
1966	73,094	73,097	−3

Figure 7.
Source: Young, Sir George. *Accommodation Services in Britain 1970-1980*, New University Education, 1970, p. 400.

It cannot be said that this is because both columns increase at a constant rate. Traffic from Sweden fell in three years, and the equation predicted two of these recessions; further, the rate of increase from 1951–6 was but a quarter of the rate of increase from 1963–7 (4·3 per cent and 17·82 per cent respectively). This pattern of increase is reflected accurately by the equation; so accurately that at the end of the period, it was only three arrivals out. A similar analysis of German arrivals in the UK showed that the derived equation was never more than 832 arrivals out in 17 years.

If advertising were such an important influence, one would expect an equation which excluded it to be a bad predictor of arrivals as it would ignore those whom the advertising campaigns tempted to the UK and who would otherwise have stayed at home or gone somewhere else.

According to the powers which they have, tourist authoritie. vary from little more than voluntary trade associations with a small staff to fully-fledged government departments with an army of civil servants headed by a minister. The trend is indisputably away from the amateur towards the professional. In spite of thi trend, the UK has no Ministry of Tourism; this is not because the requirements of the industry have been exhaustively analysed and a balanced decision taken to leave things as they are; on the con trary, it is because no such analysis has ever been undertaken and there is therefore no policy for any ministry to implement. It is the absence of a tourist policy rather than a tourist ministry that is the weakness of the UK's approach to tourism. This is not to say that the industry receives no assistance from the government; it does it is to say that such assistance is given to various components on a random basis instead of by reference to a coherent long-term policy for the industry as a whole.

The absence of this overall plan in the UK means that state-ments of intent by the British Tourist Authority become tourist policy without regard to the effect of that policy. In the *Financia. Times* supplement on hotel and catering Sir Alexander Glen, Chairman of the BTA, said 'Our marketing overseas must now be directed realistically at a target of 10–12 million visitors by 1975 and our marketing must achieve this.'[36] Why must it? Who agreed to this target? What does it imply?

The first step must be to incorporate the plans of tourist authorities with other national plans. Integration of tourist plan-ning with general planning in the UK can be achieved if res-ponsibility for tourism and for the budget of the British Tourist Authority were taken away from the Department of Trade and Industry, and handed over to the Department of the Environment. Then one department would be responsible for the promotion of tourism and for the provision for tourism through its planning functions in relation to local and regional government. An inte-grated approach would then be possible, avoiding the conflict inherent in the present situation of dual responsibility.

One should add that the UK does have a tourist infrastructure committee; but it is a sub-committee of the British Tourist Authority and it exists 'to ensure that our tourist industry enjoys a favourable climate in which to grow and flourish'.[37] This is clearly begging the question as it assumes that the tourist industry has a pre-eminent right to grow and flourish, and that the country's infrastructure should be arranged with this in mind. Ideally, the role of the tourist industry and the infrastructure necessary to support it should be the end product of a reconciliation process, taking the requirements of other activities into account. The tourist requirements should not be taken as a major input right at the beginning of the process.

The analogy with transport planning and the solution adopted in the UK is highly relevant in this context. In the days of the Ministry of Transport, road planning was a separate function from general land use planning and carried out in a different Ministry. With the absorption of the Ministry of Transport into the Department of the Environment, road planning became an integral part of the planning process and the adverse effects of road building on the environment were at any rate mitigated if not entirely eliminated. Further, new roads and by-passes were given priority if they relieved historic cities and areas of scenic value. It is this approach that is now needed with tourism. If it is not right to build urban motorways for all levels of demand for private transport – and few people would maintain that it is right – then it is equally not right to continue to develop tourist facilities for all levels of tourist demand. The machinery for restraint has therefore to be assembled.

There are fortunately signs of a more rational approach being adopted in other countries, where the need to avoid over-development is recognized and the appropriate machinery is being assembled. In Luxembourg, the Ministry of Tourism is embarking on a five-year plan, and the development proposals are linked with environmental improvements and an anti-pollution policy. The Director of the Luxembourg Tourist Office has even gone so far as to say 'It was *not* the Government's intention to encourage the building of huge new hotels as such developments often created problems. Similarly it was not policy actively to encourage congress hotels of huge proportions.'[38]

In Zambia, Mr Kazembe, the Zambian National Tourist Board's Production Officer, is on record as saying that 'Zambia realises that tourism is a highly sophisticated and delicate industry and the Government's plan is to develop a carefully planned and closely co-ordinated industry. Large groups of low-priced package tours is a short-term policy.' South Africa is likewise moving towards a centrally determined tourist policy to achieve predetermined objectives.[39] There are also hopeful signs in Yugoslavia; responsibility for the organization of tourism is being delegated to regional government, and while this will lead to slower growth, it will be of better quality and will be coordinated with other regional developments.

The British Virgin Islanders appear to have solved the problem completely.

The British Virgin Islanders have done the impossible. They have stayed a happy, friendly, welcoming colour-blind people in the maelstrom of change and progress of the modern Caribbean. They have developed rapidly, but never at the cost of selling their own souls. They have told developers 'this is the way we would like things done', and the developers have either complied or got out.[40]

In some countries, Ministries of Tourism are taking this broader view of their responsibilities. The Director of Tourism in the Dutch half of St Martin, unlike his counterparts in more 'advanced' countries, has estimated what the saturation level for tourism is, and has related this to the number of hotel beds needed to support it. His answer is 3,000, but unfortunately he lacks the legislative powers to prevent hotel building exceeding that level. Hotel proprietors are confidently predicting a 50 per cent excess, and this is an example of inadequate machinery being available to implement a sensible plan. In the same area, Bermuda is now taking a more enlightened view of its tourist industry. Michael Gregg, the Manager of the Bermuda Department of Tourism and Trade Development in London has said

... too many tourists can be a bad thing. We have found it necessary to ensure that we never have too many visitors in Bermuda at any one time by controlling the number of cruise ships that can be there together and by restricting such things as one day charter flights. It ensures that the tourist infrastructure – taxis, restaurants, sightseeing facilities etc. – does not become overloaded to the detriment of our hotel guests, on whom our livelihood depends.

At the Annual Conference of the Caribbean Travel Association in 1972, this approach was advocated by speaker after speaker, who condemned foreign hotel owners, developers and managers for their lack of knowledge of the region, for their architecture, foreign menus, lack of hospitality and high prices.[41]

If there are signs of hope in some countries, red lights are flashing in others. In Fiji for example 'One real tragedy at present is the lack of any major plan for the physical development of hotels and other necessary trappings. There are some broad outlines, but the urgent need, if the country is to avoid becoming another Honolulu, is to produce more concrete guidance and planning.'[42] Greece may be going the way of Spain and is aiming at a short-term target of 10 million visitors. *International Tourism Quarterly* had this to say about it: 'It is extremely doubtful whether Greece could cope with an influx of tourists of these dimensions even supposing that the demand potential is there, but there might be 7 million tourists before saturation point is reached – and that figure must be set against a native population of 8·7 million.'[43]

Italy would appear to be at the crossroads.

It has become increasingly clear that the traditional Italian industry, based largely on private enterprise and lacking effective State guidance and control, will soon be unable to meet the new challenge (of Spain, Greece and Yugoslavia) and that the future lies in serious State planning and investment. . . until now the tourist structure has been left to develop more or less spontaneously – a policy which has led in many places to chaos and self-damage.[44]

Contributions to the tourist industry from the State in Italy come through so many channels that they are inevitably uncoordinated and in some cases in actual conflict. There are loans for building and modernizing hotels and restaurants, grants to local and national promotional organizations and there are also funds available through Cassa per il Mezzogiorno – the development fund for the south. The government is now delegating responsibility for tourism to large regional bodies better able to coordinate the requirements and reconcile the conflicts inherent in tourism.

It is possible to over-plan and to introduce controls which are too rigid. In East Germany, one has to pre-book for a visa; and a visa to visit is only issued when a hotel bed has been reserved. The same formalities are necessary if one visits Russia, and the Russians are clearly going to have to decide quite soon how they will control their tourist industry. At the moment, they need 20,000 linguists as 'guides' for 2 million tourists, and, by all accounts, a substantial number of night porters and escorts to 'protect the tourist'. With a target of 10 million tourists by 1980, the existing ratios of guides to guests will have to give.

The time has now come for national governments to take the Goddess of Tourism off her pedestal, and to place her in the garden with all the other statues. For too long, governments have assumed unquestioningly the benefits from tourism and have encouraged it to expand. The undesirable consequences have been swept under the carpet. It is to be hoped that this decade will see a more rational and coherent approach to tourism development.

8 The Future

In this final chapter, the threads of the arguments in the preceding chapters are drawn together to see what general conclusions emerge. In the light of those conclusions, an attempt will be made to see the right way ahead and to illuminate the dangers by the wayside.

In dealing with the future of tourism, one very important point must be made clear at the outset. Previous chapters have identified two separate types of problem in connection with the growth of tourism. One problem is due to inadequate forecasting, inefficient planning and the failure to deal with the separate components of the tourist industry in a consistent and coherent way. That sort of problem is avoidable. The other one is due to the very nature and innate dynamism of tourism leading to conflicts of land use and to changes in social and economic patterns. That sort of problem is not avoidable.

There are signs that the first type of problem has been recognized and that machinery is being set up to put it right; but that machinery is not able to deal with the second type of problem – indeed, it can often make it worse – and there is a danger of creating a false sense of security as people assume that it can. This danger is made greater by the fact that the symptoms of both types of problem seem, to the inexperienced eye, to be the same.

Failure to make this crucial distinction has meant that the approach to dealing with the future of tourism has often been made on the wrong basis. It is assumed all too often that if correct demand forecasts are made and if the right number of hotels, aircraft, restaurants etc. are made available, then this is the right and indeed the only solution. But the key question for the future is no longer 'how many tourists will want to come?' but 'how many tourists do we want to welcome?' And the answer to this key question is not to be found by looking outwards at prospective visitors, but by looking inwards at prospective destinations. The fact that no ready answers are available underlines the point that the impetus of research into tourism has been largely misdirected.

Inadequate forecasts have caused so many problems in the past that it is easy, though nonetheless mistaken, to assume that correct forecasts will now put everything right. Thirty years ago planners underestimated the mobility of their fellow citizens by leaving the motorcar out of their forward thinking. Those planners are partly to blame for today's traffic congestion, parking difficulties, accidents, unreliable and expensive public transport, pedestrian inconvenience and environmental damage. But what if they had correctly forecast car ownership and car usage, and built our cities accordingly?

The role of forecasts should now be to quantify pressures rather than to indicate lines of action; for this reason it would be helpful if forecasts were right rather than wrong and to show how wide of the mark many of them have been to date, a few examples are given.

One of the earliest and most inaccurate forecasts related to car ownership. In 1939, General Motors forecast that the number of passenger cars in the USA would be 38 million in 1960.[1] In spite of America's involvement in the Second World War, this figure was exceeded by 1950. The actual figure for 1960 was 62 million. Inaccurate pre-war forecasts of car ownership were followed by equally inaccurate post-war forecasts of air travel. In 1951, the Civil Aeronautics Administration of the USA issued a forecast of domestic air travel volume in the USA for 1960 of 18 billion passenger miles. (The 1950 figure was 8 billion.) Halfway through the period, the 1960 figure had already been exceeded, and the actual 1960 figure was just over 30 billion, 66 per cent higher than that forecast. In 1962, the future was still proving as difficult to predict as ever in spite of the introduction of newer and more sophisticated forecasting techniques. In November that year the Federal Aviation Administration of the USA forecast a total of 89·5 million air passengers for the fiscal year 1967–8. The actual figure was 153 million.

This side of the Atlantic, the British Tourist Authority has con sistently underestimated the buoyancy of demand for visits to the UK. Other European countries have fared little better; in 1968, the Austrian Institute for Economic Affairs predicted that, by 1980, the gross foreign currency intake of the Austrian tourist industry would be Sch. 25,000 million (£400 million). The figure was surpassed in 1970. Unabashed, the Institute published another forecast in 1971, predicting an 80 per cent increase by 1980. This is also likely to be a hopeless underestimate. Recently the Battelle Research Centre in Geneva has started work on a world international tourist model. There are formidable problems involved, due mainly to the poor data, and the forecasts it is producing are, again, rather low.[2]

One of the conclusions from the previous two chapters was that traditional demand forecasts *should* be, in a sense, irrelevant. The chapters showed that the continued expansion of tourism at its present rate and in its present form is not a desirable phenomenon, and it follows from this that research should now be switched from forecasting to looking at methods of implementing restraint. The important issue therefore to which this final chapter addresses itself is whether one can devise a better system for administering tourism, on a national and international basis; a system which redirects or, if necessary, curbs growth; a system which gives more weight to the visited than the visitor; and which minimizes the conflicts between tourism and other national objectives.

To avoid accusations of crying wolf, one must first of all show that demand is likely to continue to increase and that tourism is not a whim of a consumer society, shortly to be replaced by something else.

The chapter on the tourist showed what strong roots demand for tourism has. Throughout the history of man, demand for travel has grown as the time and money for it became available. Over the next thirty years there is every indication of time and money becoming even more available. Travel has now assumed such a place in our way of life that the mere removal of advertising would not significantly affect the volume of travel – though it might affect its distribution. No one would seriously put forward the proposition that demand for motorcars would drop if the

manufacturers stopped advertising them, and the same considera
tion applies to travel abroad. To show how buoyant demand is, a
few selected forecasts are given.

The commission on London's third airport, The Roskill Com
mission, looked at five independent forecasts of air traffic demand
at London's airports: all five are reproduced below.[3]

Forecasting Body	Terminal Passengers (million)		
	1975	1981	1985
Research Team (Roskill Commission)	36·1	60·7	82·7
Working Party on Traffic and Capacity (Board of Trade)	32·5–40	56·4–78·6	78·5–118·5
BEA	32·3	53·4	73·4
British Airports Authority	33·9–38·2	53·9–68·2	75·7–100·2
British Airports Authority (independent consultants)	34·1	57·7	79·0

Whichever forecast is right, it is clear that demand is going to
increase by a sizeable amount. As far as overseas visitors are con
cerned, Roskill forecast 26 million in 1991 and 40 million in 2006.
This compares with 7 million overseas visitors to the UK in 1971.

One final quotation makes the same point in a different way
'An analysis of the long-term factors underlying tourist arrivals . .
suggests the continuation of the long-term growth rate . . . of
about 13 to 14 per cent over the last decade as long as US per capita
incomes increase at no less than 3 per cent annually and airfare
do not change greatly.'[4] This envisages a doubling in demand
approximately every six years. Bearing in mind that 95 per cent
of the world's population has not crossed an international frontier
and that in 1971 only one half of one per cent of the world's popu
lation did so, it is a bold man who suggests that the tourist market
is about to level off. Even as far as America is concerned, the
indication is that we are only seeing the beginning of a growing
period of increased demand.

Overall, it is clear that the US has a long way to go as a source of
tourists. In terms of consumer demand, it is probable that foreign
vacations have only scratched the surface of the vast market potential
of a huge and rich country. . . One thing is certain; all in all there will
be many more tourists and many more dollars spent in the next
decade.[5]

If another thing is certain, it is that many destinations have not got the capacity to absorb those Americans, or indeed the many other travellers. The resolution of this conflict lies in a radical change in the role of the principal players in what has the makings of an excellent Greek drama. There are six of them, as follows: international government, national government, tourist authorities, local government (including residents), the tourist and the tourist industry.

As far as international government is concerned, there is no machinery yet available for implementing any international tourist policy. However, this is no reason for not looking at what its role should be; indeed, until a case is made for that role, no machinery will be made available. In broad terms, it should seek to optimize tourist flows on an international basis, for the same reasons and, to some extent in the same way, as the World Bank might optimize currency flows. It has been admitted by IUOTO that the present system whereby each of its members tries to cope individually with the tourist phenomenon is not sustainable. 'It will be impossible to meet world tourism demands at its present rate of development without new forms of international planning.'[6] The same view has been put forward by the Director-General of IATA: 'This [increase in tourism] should serve as a reminder that somewhere there may be a limit to tourist development along present lines'.[7] Nowadays, no one would seriously put forward the proposition that the planning of a country's motorway or rail network should be in the hands of each component local authority, each being free to build sections of track or road as best suited local needs, and to carry such traffic as it wished. National transport is rightly the concern and responsibility of national government; yet what about international transport? The logic of the argument, and indeed the reality of today's needs, require international government to plan for the future. As long as each country continues to try to secure for itself a growing share of a tourist market, an international approach based on optimizing tourist flows between countries will not be possible. Countries which would be better off without so many tourists will suffer, as will those countries who could usefully have some more. By redirecting tourist flows away from countries under pressure towards those with

spare capacity, a world tourist authority could do on an inte
national scale what national planning agencies already do on
smaller scale, for example, by selecting areas within a country
accommodate population growth. All that is suggested therefo
is an extension of planning powers which already exist national
to deal with an essentially international phenomenon.

Such an authority could also take the initiative in removing th
existing subsidies to the tourist industry in all the countries co
cerned. It has been shown that this distorts national economie
can penalize other industries with better export performances an
it also constitutes a regressive tax on the poorer non-travellin
ratepayer and taxpayer. In the same way as GATT and the EE
prohibit subsidies to certain industries, so a world tourist authori
could bring some common sense to the administrations co
cerned, each of which is scared to take unilateral action for fear
losing a competitive advantage on price.

An international body is likewise necessary to safeguard touri
resources, such as the Mediterranean, which belong to no on
country and which are being destroyed by short-sighted and selfis
national policies. It might also be able to save tourist attraction
acknowledged to be international assets, which might otherwi
be lost through shortage of national funds. By the end of th
century, a world airline is a distinct possibility, and this could
the instrument for implementing any international policies tha
had been agreed.

The emergence of a world tourist authority to perform the
tasks may well be a long way off. But in other fields internation
bodies with growing powers are emerging, able to take a glob
view of problems and able to implement solutions; and, increa
ingly, countries are prepared to surrender sovereignty to the
bodies in the belief that a wider public good is served by so doin
Inevitably, a development along these lines would be portraye
as an unwarranted intrusion on the freedom of the individual to g
where he likes when he likes; this accusation would be made if,
is likely, tourist quotas are introduced for many countries.
would also be opposed by those with an instinctive dislike of an
form of planning. But what is the alternative; to continue with th
present system and let many tourist cities grind to a halt? to se

them completely altered by trying to absorb a growing number of visitors and, inevitably, becoming different cities as a result? If the United States of America need a national recreational policy, will not the United States of Europe? The restrictions proposed, in the interest of society as a whole, are no worse in reality than the planning restrictions which forbid development in certain parts of the country; and few people would dispute that what that legislation has preserved was worth preserving; indeed public opinion would support the proposition that the legislation had not gone far enough.

A world tourist authority would provide the framework within which national government could tackle the problem of tourism in its own particular country. The relevant chapter of this book has argued for a change in the machinery of government to remove certain privileges from the tourist industry which it currently enjoys in many countries. The reasons for those privileges in many cases were never valid, and in others are no longer so. It was argued that tourism should be placed on an equal footing with other industries, and that plans for tourism should be more closely integrated with other national plans. Government should acknowledge the existence of conflicts between the growth of tourism and other national objectives, and should devise machinery to minimize it.

As far as the UK is concerned, this approach is dependent on the prior transferral of responsibility for tourism from the Department of Trade and Industry to the Department of the Environment. If this were done, it would then be possible to harness the energies of the tourist industry in a more beneficial way, in particular by directing the tourist's expenditure towards conservation of historic areas and generating activity in those parts of the country which need it. The Department of the Environment, through its other powers, would be able to minimize the special brand of pollution which tourism creates – traffic jams, crowds, noise, fumes and litter, which so often destroy the very things tourists come to see. Through its overall responsibility for local government, the Department of the Environment would be able to provide the link which is currently missing – between the promotional activities of the British Tourist Authority overseas and the provision of tourist facilities in the areas which are visited. It is this absence of coordination, of overall responsibility, which is the most disturbing feature of the tourist scene in the UK at the moment. The problem has arisen because the Department of Trade and Industry is the sponsor department for tourism, but the Department of the Environment is the government department responsible for planning. The Department of Trade and Industry encourages hoteliers to build hotels by providing grants of £1,000 per room, but the Department of the Environment turns down many of the planning applications on appeal. This summarizes, in a nutshell, the result of having two government departments responsible for tourism. If one wishes to relate tourist flows to tourist infrastructure, to relate the capacity of airports to the capacity of tourist regions, then one must have one department with overall responsibility and the Department of the Environment is more likely to take an enlightened view of its responsibilities in this matter than the Department of Trade and Industry.

If the supply of tourist facilities is to be restricted through government action, it may be necessary for government to intervene in another way, namely through control of hotel prices. If the number of hotel rooms in London is limited for strategic planning reasons, then there will be a shortage of hotel beds relative to demand, and a danger of prices escalating until supply and demand are in balance. To prevent the abuse of a monopoly position, governments may well have to control hotel prices. In France and Spain, the first steps towards price control of hotels have already been taken and in Greece the government controls the price of hotel meals, and it is an offence to add on any additional taxes or tips. The introduction of hotel registration in the UK could provide the means for price control should it become necessary for government to intervene in this way.

It is interesting to note that this course of action has already been advocated by the Director General of IATA, Mr Knut Hammarskold. He argues[8] that since price control through IATA has resulted in a 40 per cent reduction in tariffs over ten years, price control should therefore be extended to other sections of the industry that had not, in his view, been as attentive to the needs of the consumer. While one might disagree with the logic of his argument – without I A T A, tariffs would never have been so high, or they would have fallen even faster – one is inclined to accept the conclusion, that without price control the interests of the consumer might be overlooked by the accommodation industry.

This will mean a new role for tourist authorities or Ministries of tourism. Instead of being promotional bodies aimed at securing a maximum tourist flow, they are more likely to become tourist development corporations over the next two decades, acting within the context of a national plan which identifies the role of tourism and which blends the requirement of the tourist with that of the resident. In many cases, the traditional promotional campaigns will be dismantled, and in some cases, actually reversed: 'Please don't come to Britain this year.' The financial incentives payable to the tourist industry through tourist authorities are also likely to be removed and, in some cases, reversed as saturation levels are approached. Where these levels have been exceeded, fiscal incentives may well be replaced by penal taxes in order to get the level of tourist activity down to an acceptable level by pricing out the weakest hotels. In short, the terms of reference of tourist authorities are likely to be changed. Instead of going out to the highways and byways and compelling them to come in, they will be asked to be more selective in their activities, and to be more aware of the needs of the host.

The initiative for many of the changes which are needed will have to come from local government; for it is at that level that the problems dealt with in this book first manifest themselves, and it is at this level that the need for a solution is most pressing. Quite simply, the supply of accommodation will not be able to keep pace with the increase in demand in those destinations where land is already at a premium. For example, 90 per cent of all overseas visitors to the UK spend some time in London, and 75 per cent of these go nowhere else. In spite of repeated attempts to alter this distribution, it has remained obdurately constant. The capacity of London to continue to absorb annual increases of around 13 per cent in visitor traffic is limited, notwithstanding the protestations of the BTA to the contrary. If an extra 1 million visitors come to London each year for ten nights, and their visits are evenly spread throughout the year, then, even if only 30 per cent of those nights are spent in hotels, an extra 8,000 hotel beds are needed each year. While this amount of accommodation can be provided for most of the current decade, the land simply is not available thereafter. The same restrictions will apply to other historic centres such as Paris and Rome. The question is not whether tourism to centres such as these continues to grow at the present rate, because it cannot. The key question is at what level should it be contained and how. The answer lies in the identification of maximum levels of tourist demand which can be accommodated, and the use of the planning mechanism to restrict demand to that level through such means as hotel quotas etc. It is fortunate that local government in the UK is being reorganized into larger and stronger units, which are more likely to finance the necessary research and to identify the necessary solutions. Further, these larger units are more likely to press for the implementation of these solutions against a government which might not be so willing to accept them. Work initiated by the Greater London Council[9] and by the Westminster City Council[10] shows how suspicious local authorities are now becoming about the benefits of tourist growth and, increasingly, in the next decade there will be clashes between bodies such as those and the tourist industry.

As far as the tourist himself is concerned, he may find himself less welcome than he was in the past; he may find prices rising faster as tourist subsidies are withdrawn; and he will certainly find that his freedom to go where he wants when he wants is substantially reduced. This will be due to the increase in tourist numbers exceeding the extra capacity likely to be forthcoming and because the growth in numbers is a threat to the environment and values of those he wishes to visit. 'The tourist, in his search for something different, inevitably erodes and destroys that difference by his very enjoyment of it.'[11]

Distance will become less important as an influence in the choice of the tourist's destination. Longer holidays, reductions in the real cost of air travel and faster aircraft will mean that destinations currently excluded from his range of choice will be included. The West Indies, the Pacific and the Far East will be popular tourist destinations for Europeans. Second holidays, many taken in the winter, will be another growth area where it may be less necessary to impose restrictions because of excess capacity in those months.

Hopes that the tourist of the future will be a more sensitive and appreciative creature, respective of local cultures and anxious not to upset the natives, may not be fulfilled. The growth in tourist numbers will be provided by those who are not aware of the sort of problems with which this book is concerned and therefore they will not be able to mitigate the ill effects which they, albeit unconsciously, may cause. There is, in fact, every sign that the tourist will replace the motorist as the environmentalist's Aunt Sally.

The tourist industry faces increased governmental supervision over the next two decades; this will partly be due to its ever increasing size and influence; partly due to the need to draw up and implement a tourist plan in the context of broader national plans; partly in response to public opinion insisting on higher standards, both physically and ethically; and partly due to the need to curb monopoly profits.

This growing governmental involvement is visible in the UK. Registration of hotels under the auspices of the English Tourist Board is under way; the government has passed legislation which enables the Civil Aviation Authority to license tour operators; there are frequent attempts in parliament to replace the ineffective sanctions used by the Association of British Travel Agents to discipline their members with something more punitive; the Consumer Association is pressing for legislation on car-hire firms. In short, the freedom of the tourist industry to behave as it wishes will be curbed in the UK, and many of the measures envisaged are already in force overseas.

Within this more orderly and, arguably more restrictive framework the structure of the industry will continue to change. Within countries, airlines will continue to merge to produce viable units and, internationally, national airlines will merge as patriotism is replaced by economic logic as the major influence. Aircraft travel will become more like bus and train travel; booking may gradually disappear and fares may be paid during or immediately before flight. The effect of these developments on cost and hence on demand could be dramatic. For instance, air travel from London to Edinburgh on a no booking night flight is cheaper than the train journey. The structure of air-fares will change until the unhelpful distinction between scheduled and charter flights disappears. The present situation whereby scheduled flights become less popular and therefore more expensive, and charter flights become more popular and therefore cheaper is not sustainable indefinitely, and the scheduled airlines will invade the charter market to maintain their load factors. Fewer types of aircraft will be manufactured, leading to economies of scale and rationalization of servicing and repair arrangements. More and larger airports will be needed, but they will be sited away from the centres of population and utilize modern technology to transport passengers from the airports to their destinations. It may even be possible to close the second generation airports close to the city centres and use the land for more suitable purposes. The first generation airports e.g. Croydon and Hendon in London have already been closed.

The numbers of travel agents will contract steadily, leaving only the larger and more efficient in operation, together with the retail outlets owned by the travel conglomerates. The number of tour operators will likewise decline until the largest three or four account for about 80 per cent of the market. More and more reservations will be done by mail order and telephone, with computerized reservation schemes giving immediate response to availability enquiries. Hotel reservation systems will merge to form one network covering most hotels, replacing the existing arrangements whereby more than one system cover some hotels. The closing down in 1972 by International Reservations Ltd of its UK booking system is an instance of this trend. The industrial logic which led to the merging of rival telephone, rail and water companies applies equally to hotel reservation systems; it is a waste of resources to duplicate the service and it is confusing to the customer. The industry will also continue to integrate vertically so that many of the components of a complicated package will be provided by one large travel conglomerate. Should these conglomerates become too large, they may be restricted by legislation on the lines of American anti-trust legislation.

To conclude, the future of tourism represents a serious challenge to man's ability to organize himself; to succeed, present attitudes towards tourism and current methods of planning for it must change; and they must change in a way which neither the tourist nor the tourist industry may appreciate.

Those who instigate these changes, for the long-term benefit of society – including the tourist – will stand accused of curbing man's freedom to travel and of restricting the liberty of the individual and of private enterprise. Such a criticism is short-sighted as it ignores the damage that unrestrained tourist development can cause and assumes that no price for freedom of movement can be too high. It is that view, above all else, that must be changed.

References

Chapter 2

1. 1 Kings x.
2. Norval, A. J., *The Tourist Industry*, Sir Isaac Pitman & Sons, 1936, p. 23.
3. Pimlott, J. A. R., *The Englishman's Holiday*, Faber & Faber, 1947, p. 23.
4. Lennard, Reginald et al., *Englishmen at Rest and Play, 1558–1714*, Wadham College, 1931.
5. Pimlott, J. A. R., op. cit., p. 55.
6. ibid., p. 191.
7. The *Manchester Guardian*, 6 August 1855.
8. Pimlott, J. A. R., op. cit., p. 191.
9. Gruntzel, *Economic Protectionism*, pp. 116–17.
10. Alkjaer, Prof., and Eriksen, Jorn L., *Location and Economic Consequences of International Congresses*, Einar Harcks Forlag, Copenhagen, 1967, p. 9.
11. Brunner, Elizabeth, *Holidaymaking and the Holiday Trades*, Oxford University Press, 1945, p. 11.
12. White, Arthur, *Palaces of the People*, Rapp & Whiting, 1968, p. 164.
13. Huxley, A., *Along the Road*, 1925.
14. Cmd 1636, HMSO, 1935.
15. Norval, A. J., op. cit., p. 48.
16. Ogilvie, F. W., *The Tourist Movement*, P. S. King & Son Ltd, 1933, p. 14a.
17. *The Times*, 22 September 1931.
18. *The Times*, 14 April 1932.
19. Ogilvie, F. W., op. cit., p. 14a.
20. *Bulletin de l'institut Internationale Statistique*, Tome XXIV, Deuxième Livraison, p. 32, Tome XXIII, Première Livraison, p. 96.
21. Ogilvie, F. W., op. cit., p. 30.
22. ibid., p. 36.

Chapter 3

1. Arthur D. Little, Inc., *Tourism and Recreation*, October 1967, table 5–2, p. 64.
2. *British National Travel Survey, 1967*, British Tourist Authority, 1967, table 24, p. 6.
3. Outdoor Recreation Resources Review Commission, *Report no. 20*, Washington DC, 1962, p. 49.
4. *Research Newsletter no. 3*, British Tourist Authority, Winter 1971, p. 6.
5. *British National Travel Survey*, op. cit., table 31, p. 33.
6. Zedek, Dr Gustav, and Prunster, Dr Josef, *Konjunkturelle und strukturelle Aspekte des Österreichischen Fremdenverkehrs*, Schriftenreihe der Bundeskammer der gewerblichen Wirtschaft, February 1967, p. 7.
7. See note 5; and Young, Sir George, *Accommodation Services in Britain, 1970–1980*, New University Education, 1970, p. 176.
8. Owen, Wilfred, *Strategy for Mobility*, Brookings Institute, Washington DC, 1964, p. 14.
9. Waters, S. R., 'Trends in International Tourism', *Development Digest*, vol. V, no. 2, Washington DC.
10. Economic Planning Staff, 'Overseas Development Administration', *Project Data Handbook – Tourism*, Foreign and Commonwealth Office, London, March 1972, p. 53.
11. ORRRC, Report no. 20, op. cit., table 37, p. 41.
12. *British National Travel Survey*, op. cit., table 36, p. 156.
13. International Labour Convention, 53rd Session, *Holidays with Pay*, Geneva, 1969, Report 6, para. 82.
14. *British National Travel Survey, 1955*, (Later BNTS omit this data) British Tourist Authority, 1955.
15. ORRRC, *Report no. 20*, op. cit., tables 36 and 37, pp. 40–41.
16. *A Report on Recreation and Tourism in the Loch Lomond Area*, University of Glasgow, June 1968, Appendix 1.
17. *British National Travel Survey, 1967*, op. cit., table 32, p. 34.
18. ORRRC, *Report no. 20*, op. cit., p. 52.
19. Travel Research International Inc., *Vacation Travel Attitude Survey* (An original research project jointly sponsored by Air Travel Magazine, American Airlines, Eastern Airlines, National Geographic and Transworld Airlines), June 1967, Fig. 6.
20. *British National Travel Survey, 1967*, op. cit., table 29, p. 31.
21. ibid., table 30, p. 32.

22. *Employment and Productivity Gazette*, vol. LXXVII, no. 6, June 1969, table 129, p. 606.

23. 'Products and People. A digest of the Marketing Survey of the European Common Market and Britain', *Readers Digest*, 1963, table 35.

24. Government Social Survey, *Motives in the Timing of Holidays*, HMSO, 1961, table 40b.

25. Travel Research International Inc., op. cit.

26. *British National Travel Survey, 1967*, op. cit., table 25, p. 27.

27. Knebel, H. J., *Soziologische Strukturwandlungen im modernen Tourismus*, Stuttgart, 1960.

28. Dichter, Dr Ernst, 'What motivates people to travel?', Address to the Department of Tourism of the Government of Inida, Kashmir, October 1967.

29. Lansing, John B., and Blood, Dwight M., *The Changing Travel Market*, Survey Research Center, Institute for Social Research, The University of Michigan, Ann Arbor, Michigan, p. 11.

30. Travel Research International Inc., op. cit.

31. Lansing, John B., op. cit., p. 11.

32. *Research Newsletter no. 3*, op. cit., p. iii.

33. *Travel and Leisure Research*, a survey carried out for the BTA in 1972.

34. *Research Newsletter no. 3*, op. cit., table 3.

35. Schmidhauser, Dr H. et al, *Untersuchung über den Fremdenverkehr in Stadt Zürich*, Seminar für Fremdenverkehr an der Hochschule St Gallen, 1968, p. 39.

36. Young, Sir George, op. cit., p. 47.

37. Blomstrom, Robert L., *The Commercial Lodging Market*, Phase II, Market Research Project, American Hotel, Restaurant and Institutional Management, Graduate School of Business Administration, Michigan State University, East Lansing, Library of Congress Catalog Card no. 67–65501, tables IV–1, IV–18.

38. Industrial Market Research Ltd, *The Business Use of Hotel Services and Amenities in the UK*, presented to NEDO 1969, vol. II, pp. 7–16, 7–23.

39. 'Those Nights away from Home', *British Agents Review*, April 1968.

40. Blomstrom, Robert, op. cit., table II–31, p. 43.

41. Zedek, Dr Gustav, *Der Fremdenverkehr in der Osterreichischen Wirtschaft*, Bundeskammer der gewerblichen Wirtschaft, Vienna.

42. Alkjaer, Prof., *Memorandum on the case for the Covent Garden Centre*, Institute for Transport, Tourism and Regional Science, The Copenhagen School of Business Administration, June 1972, p. 7.

43. Alkjaer, Prof., and Eriksen, Jorn L., *Location and Economic Conse-quences of International Congresses*, Einar Harcks Forlag, Copen-hagen, 1967, pp. 9–10.
44. Young, Sir George, op. cit., p. 481.

Chapter 4

1. *Economic Review of World Tourism*, IUOTO, Geneva, 1972, pp. 7, 8.
2. 'International Tourism', *Quarterly Economic Review*, Special number 7, Economist Intelligence Unit, 1970, p. 23.
3. *Economic Review of World Tourism*, op. cit., p. 9.
4. *Economic Review of World Tourism*, IUOTO, 1970.
5. *Economic Review of World Tourism*, 1972, op. cit., p. 9.
6. *Tourism in OECD Member Countries*, Organisation for Economic Co-operation and Development, Paris, 1970.
7. Figures from successive OECD publications.
8. ibid., pp. 23–4.
9. ibid., .p 28.
10. ibid., p. 16.
11. *International Passenger Surveys*, 1964–71, Department of Trade and Industry; and *Business Monitor M6*, November 1972.
12. Home Office Immigration Statistics.
13. *Digest of Tourist Statistics*, British Tourist Authority, 1971, p. 13.
14. *Economic Trends*, Central Statistics Office.
15. *Business Monitor M6*, op. cit.
16. *Digest of Tourist Statistics*, op. cit., pp. 54–5.
17. ibid., p. 63.
18. ibid., pp. 54–5.
19. Home Office Statistics.
20. Young, Sir George, *Accommodation Services in Britain, 1970–80*, New University Education, 1970, pp. 439–43.
21. ibid., pp. 47, 610, 641.
22. ibid., p. 412.
23. ibid., p. 47.
24. *Digest of Tourist Statistics*, op. cit., p. 65.
25. *British Home Tourism*, British Tourist Authority, 1972.
26. Government Social Survey, *Motives in the Timing of Holidays*, HMSO, 1961.
27. Annual Abstract of Statistics, HMSO, 1971.
28. *Digest of Tourist Statistics*, op. cit., p. 68.
29. ibid., 1972, p. 69.

30. ibid., p. 69.
31. *International Passenger Surveys*, 1966–71, op. cit.; and *Business Monitor M6*, op. cit.

Chapter 5

1. *Travel Trade Gazette*, 3 September 1971.
2. *Travel Trade Gazette*, 13 October 1972.
3. The *Sunday Times*, 25 April 1972.
4. *Travel Trade Gazette*, 31 December 1971.
5. *Travel Trade Gazette*, 21 April 1972.
6. *The Times*, 9 November 1972.
7. Cmd 6712, *British Air Services*, HMSO, 1945.
8. Cmnd 1457, *Civil Aerodromes and Air Navigational Services*.
9. Cmnd 4018, *British Air Transport in the Seventies*.
10. ibid., para. 904.
11. ibid., para. 892.
12. *First Report of the Select Committee on Nationalised Industries*, British Airports Authority, Session 1970–71, p. XV.
13. Cmnd 1824, *Report of Committee of Inquiry into the Major Ports of Great Britain*, 1962.
14. ibid., paras. 140 and 151.
15. Cmnd 4018, op. cit., para. 897.
16. ibid., para. 1013.
17. ibid., para. 71.
18. *Pollution, Nuisance or Nemesis?*, a report on the control of pollution, HMSO, February 1972, para. 236.
19. The *Sunday Times*, 28 May 1972.
20. Cmnd 4018, op. cit., para. 912.
21. *The British Airports Authority, Annual Report and Accounts, 1970–71*, HMSO, p. 30.
22. The *Financial Times*, 4 August 1971.
23. Cmnd 4018, op. cit., para. 911.
24. *Business Monitor CA2*, June 1971.
25. *World Air Transport Statistics*, 17th ed., International Air Transport Association, 1973.
26. Cmnd 4018, op. cit., para. 13.
27. *The Times*, 1 June 1972.
28. The *Financial Times*, 29 September 1972.
29. John Savage, Managing Director of Britannia Airways, *Travel Trade Gazette*, 8 October 1971.
30. The *Financial Times*, 29 September 1972.

31. The *New York Times*, 2 October 1972.
32. The *Financial Times*, 25 November 1971.
33. *Trade and Industry*, HMSO, 14 September 1972, p. 45.
34. *Hotels and Tourism in Westminster*, City of Westminster, 1972, para. 6.5 (vi).
35. *Unwanted Visitors*, a report on the Emergency Accommodation Scheme run by Christian Action for young visitors during the summer of 1970, Christian Action Publications, 104 Newgate Street London EC1.
36. *Hotels and Tourism in Westminster*, op. cit., para. 8.2(i).
37. The *Financial Times*, 9 October 1971.
38. *Hotels and Tourism in Westminster*, op. cit., 11.3(i).
39. ibid., Appendix G, 2(a).

Chapter 6

1. Young, Sir George, *Accommodation Services in Britain, 1970–1980*, New University Education, 1970, p. 663.
2. Greater London Development Plan Inquiry *Support Paper S 111–9*, Greater London Council, October 1971.
3. *Hotels and Tourism*, Topic Paper T 1, City of Westminster, Westminster City Hall, May 1972, para. 7.6(iii).
4. *Tourism and Hotels in London – a Paper for Discussion*, Greater London Council, March 1971, para. 5.13.
5. *Hotels and Tourism*, op. cit., para. 8.3(vii and ix).
6. ibid., para. 8.3(vi).
7. 'The Visitor Industry and Hawaii's Economy: A Cost-Benefit Analysis', *Mathematica*, Princeton, 1970, p. 3.
8. The *Financial Times*, Supplement on the Cayman Islands, 17 September 1971.
9. *Hotels and Tourism*, op. cit., paras. 2.1, 3.1(ii).
10. ibid., para. 12.1(ii).
11. *Planning for Amenity and Tourism*, An Foras Forbartha, Dublin, 1966.
12. *Hotels and Tourism*, op. cit., para. 11.3(i).
13. Economic Planning Staff, 'Overseas Development Administration', *Project Data Handbook – Tourism*, Foreign and Commonwealth Office, London, March 1972, p. 71.
14. See Chapter 4, pp. 58–60.
15. *Architectural Review*, September 1972.
16. *Hotels and Tourism*, op. cit., para. 12.2(ii).
17. Economic Planning Staff, op. cit., p. 58.

18. *New Society*, 18 May 1972.
19. *Hotels and Tourism*, op. cit., para. 10.3(vi).
20. For example, Private Member's bill introduced in the House of Lords by the Royal Borough of Kensington and Chelsea, 1971–2 Parliamentary Session.
21. *Tourism and Hotels in London*, op. cit., p. 30.
22. Janin, B., 'Tourisme dans les grandes Alpes Italiennes', *Revue Geographique des Alpes*, 1964.
23. Cosgrove, Isobel, and Jackson, R., *The Geography of Recreation and Leisure*, Hutchinson, 1972, p. 127.
24. The *Financial Times*, 20 January 1970.
25. Lundberg, Donald, *The Tourist Business*, Institution/VFM Books, Chicago 1972, p. 141.
26. *Tourism and Hotels in London*, op. cit., p. 34.
27. Cosgrove, Isobel, op. cit., p. 59.

Chapter 7

1. *Travel Trade Gazette*, 19 May 1972.
2. Economic Planning Staff, 'Overseas Development Administration', *Project Data Handbook – Tourism*, Foreign and Commonwealth Office, London, March 1972, p. 63.
3. English Tourist Board, *Annual Report and Accounts for the Year ended 31 March 1972*, p. 63.
4. The *Financial Times*, 25 May 1972.
5. The *Financial Times*, 19 November 1972.
6. Economic Planning Staff, op. cit., p. 72.
7. Stockholm Enskilda Bank, *Some Data about Sweden*, 1971, table 23.
8. *Travel Trade Gazette*, 1 September 1972.
9. *Travel Trade Gazette*, 5 November 1971.
10. The *New York Times*, 9 August 1970.
11. Renucci, J., 'La Corse et le Tourisme', *Revue Geographique de Lyon*, p. 207.
12. Levitt Kari and Gulati Iqbal, 'Income Effect of Tourist Spending; Mystification multiplied; a critical comment on the Zinder Report', *Social and Economic Studies*, September 1970; and Economic Planning Staff, op. cit., p. 3.
13. Zinder and Associates, *The Future of Tourism in the Eastern Caribbean*, May 1969.
14. Checci and Co., 'Multiplier Analysis' from *A Plan for managing the Growth of Tourism in the Commonwealth of the Bahama Islands*, Washington DC, 1969, appendix 3.

15. The *Financial Times*, 16 May 1972; and University of Strathclyde Survey.
16. Mitchell F., *The Costs and Benefits of Tourism in Kenya*, Report to the Kenya Tourist Development Corporation, Nairobi, 1968, p. 3.
17. *Wall Street Journal*, 24 August 1970.
18. Economic Planning Staff, op. cit., p. 3.
19. Roman Manuel, *The Limits of Economic Growth in Spain*, Praeger Special Studies in International Economics, Praeger Publishers, 1971, p. 51.
20. Economic Planning Staff, op. cit., p. 77.
21. The *Financial Times*, 18 May 1972.
22. *Travel Trade Gazette*, 13 October 1972.
23. Economic Planning Staff, op. cit., p. 75.
24. Economist Intelligence Unit Ltd, *International Tourism Quarterly*, Report no. 1, 1972, p. 43.
25. Economic Planning Staff, op. cit., p. 88.
26. Government of Israel, *Investors Guide to Tourism*, Tel Aviv, 1968.
27. The *Financial Times*, 22 May 1972.
28. The *Financial Times*, 25 September 1971.
29. 'Europe's Majestic Sewer', *New Scientist*, 26 October 1972, p. 195.
30. *New Scientist and Science Journal*, 15 July 1971, p. 144.
31. *The Times*, 7 September 1972.
32. The *Evening Standard*, 23 March 1972.
33. Greater London Council, *Greater London Development Plan Statement*, para. 9.4.
34. *Public Money in the Private Sector*, 6th Report from Expenditure Committee, Session 1971–2, Questions 2499–2517, HMSO, July 1972.
35. Economic Planning Staff, op. cit., p. 58.
36. The *Financial Times*, 4 January 1971.
37. *Board of Trade Journal*, 23 September 1970.
38. *Travel Trade Gazette*, 28 April 1972.
39. The *Financial Times*, 14 June 1971.
40. The *Financial Times*, 21 May 1971.
41. *Travel Trade Gazette*, 6 October 1972.
42. The *Financial Times*, 7 October 1971.
43. Economist Intelligence Unit Ltd, *International Tourism Quarterly*, Issue no. 1, 1971, p. 8.
44. *The Times*, 26 February 1971.

Chapter 8

1. Outdoor Recreation Resources Review Commission, *Projections to the Years 1976 and 2000*, (ORRRC Study Report 23), Library of Congress Catalog Card Number 62–60045, Washington DC, 1962, p. 75.
2. Armstrong C. W. G., 'International Tourism – Coming or Going? The methodological problems of forecasting', *Future*, vol. 4, no. 2, IPC Science and Technology Press Ltd, UK, pp. 115–25.
3. *Report of the Commission on London's Third Airport*, appendix 6, table 8, HMSO, 1971.
4. Economic Planning Staff, 'Overseas Development Administration', *Project Data Handbook – Tourism*, Foreign and Commonwealth Office, London, March 1972, p. 88.
5. *International Tourism Quarterly*, no. 2, EIU Ltd, 1972, p. 69.
6. *Travel Trade Gazette*, 10 September 1971.
7. *Travel Trade Gazette*, 6 October 1972.
8. *Travel Trade Gazette*, 10 March 1972.
9. *Tourism and Hotels in London – A Paper for Discussion*, Greater London Council, March 1971.
10. *Summary Paper on Hotels and Tourism*, Topic Paper T1, City of Westminster, May 1972.
11. Cosgrove, Isobel, and Jackson, Richard, *The Geography of Recreation and Leisure*, Hutchinson, 1972.